D0592703

LEND
A
HAND

THE HOW, WHERE, AND WHY OF VOLUNTEERING

Mid-Valley School District
Senior High School Library

LEND
—A—
HAND

THE HOW, WHERE, AND WHY OF VOLUNTEERING

SARA GILBERT

MORROW JUNIOR BOOKS / NEW YORK

Copyright © 1988 by Sara Gilbert
All rights reserved.
No part of this book may be reproduced
or utilized in any form or by any means,
electronic or mechanical, including
photocopying, recording or by any information
storage and retrieval system,
without permission in writing from the Publisher.
Inquiries should be addressed to
William Morrow and Company, Inc.,
105 Madison Avenue,
New York, NY 10016.

Printed in the United States of America.
1 2 3 4 5 6 7 8 9 10

Library of Congress Cataloging-in-Publication Data
Gilbert, Sara
Lend a hand: the how, where, and why
of volunteering/Sara Gilbert.
p.   cm.
Summary: Lists voluntary organizations which perform a wide
variety of useful services and which welcome the assistance of young
people, and explains how worthwhile it is to "get involved."
ISBN 0-688-07247-X
1. Voluntarism—United States—Directories—Juvenile literature.
2. Associations, institutions, etc.—United States—Directories—
Juvenile literature. [1. Voluntarism—Directories.] I. Title.
HN90.V64G55 1988
361.3'7'02573—dc19   87-32077   CIP   AC

"If I am not for myself, who am I?
If I am not for others, what am I?
If not now, when?"

—HILLEL

CONTENTS

III. HOW TO VOLUNTEER

ACKNOWLEDGMENTS

The author gratefully acknowledges the contributions of all of the organizations that responded generously to her requests for information for this book, and expresses special thanks to The Georgetown Day High School and The Sidwell Friends School, of Washington, D.C., for their help.

AUTHOR'S NOTE

In order to gather information for this book, the author wrote to over 250 nonprofit organizations whose names were collected from *The Encyclopedia of Associations* and other sources. Every effort was made to select a thorough roster for each category— one that represented a variety of views of, and approaches to, a particular problem.

A second, more urgent, letter was sent to those groups that did not respond to the first. The one hundred-plus organizations listed here are those that ultimately responded. The author regrets if any sections do not seem absolutely complete or fully "well-rounded," but she feels strongly that any nonresponsive organizations should not be included.

Readers should note that the **information included in the entries was provided by the organizations themselves,** and was accurate at the time the book was prepared for publication.

Finally, readers who do not find groups to meet their interests within these pages are urged to pursue additional information from the resources included in pages 140–152 and elsewhere throughout the book.

THIS BOOK IS FOR YOU

If you are one of the *many* **young people** who, for whatever reason, want to connect with the people of your community or the world, with your life today—and tomorrow . . .

If you are a **youth counselor** in need of ideas for channeling the energy and talent of the young people you guide . . .

If you are part of an **organization** seeking creative ways to perform service . . .

Then this book will help you to *lend a hand.*

Lend a Hand lists voluntary organizations that perform a wide variety of useful services and that welcome the assistance of young people. Those listed by name here were chosen from a large body of recognized and established service groups and are included on the basis of their responses to written inquiries for letters and material describing their activities. You'll want to ask your own questions of any group to which you decide to lend your hand, but these lists should get you started, as will the other suggestions for worthwhile volunteering that you'll find throughout the book.

Is volunteering "worthwhile"? That may be the first question you will ask yourself—and you'll have a chance to think about that one, beginning with Chapter 1.

PART
ONE

WHY VOLUNTEER?

ONE

WHY LEND YOUR HAND?

All of these people are looking for *something more* in their lives. Which one is most like you?

Tony is determined to become a doctor, and he can't wait to get started. Beth loves animals, but she can't have pets in her apartment. Alison has her heart set on a top-rated university, but her grades and test scores aren't outstanding enough. Ken must meet a community service requirement for his school, and has no idea what to do. Music is all that matters to Richard— he can't seem to enjoy anything else. Rachel thinks she might want to be a teacher, but she needs more facts before she can decide for sure. Tim is just looking for a more interesting way to spend his summer than working in the local hamburger joint. Vinnie is frustrated and frightened by what he sees in the world, and he wishes he could *do* something about it.

How can each of these very different people find the "something more" they need and want? By *volunteering*—by lending their hands to service that gets them involved with their world and the people in it.

This book is about how, why, and where to volunteer. The following chapters are filled with ideas and suggestions about *how* and *where* to volunteer.

This chapter is about *why*.

Why volunteer? Let's go back to our opening examples: Tony can work without pay at a hospital or medical center, and begin his "medical career" right now. Beth can volunteer at an animal shelter or animal-protection organization to satisfy her love for animals. Alison, by volunteering, can create a special image of herself that will look fine on a college application. Ken can use this list and other resources to find a satisfying way to fill his school's requirement. Richard can fill his days with music by joining—or organizing—a community orchestra, by playing for local hospitals or schools, or by volunteering to teach music. Rachel can see what teaching is like by helping out in a nursery school or day camp. Tim can spend a nonboring summer by getting involved with any group anywhere in the world that's doing something that interests him. Vinnie can offer his services to any of literally thousands of local, state, national, and international organizations and agencies that work toward solutions of the world's many problems.

By doing "something more" right now, all of these people can find something more for themselves—for now and for later.

When you lend your hand, you give something important to the world around you, and you also gain something important for yourself. It's easy to see what you *give*, but it may not be so easy to see what you *gain*.

DOING GOOD . . .

We don't have to look far to see the troubles of the world: The hungry, the homeless, and the addicted may be just outside our windows; disease, death, illiteracy, and impending world de-

Mid-Valley School District
Senior High School Library

struction are as close as our television screens. The needs sometimes seem so massive that as individuals we feel despair: "What can *I* do about it?!"

We can do something about even the most overwhelming crisis if each of us joins with others to make a contribution.

It's not just the growing size of our world's and our community's problems that make "doing good" more important than ever before. It's also that the resources available to deal with those problems are growing smaller: Changes in our social patterns and our economic system mean that there are fewer people with time and money to spare for these efforts. So everybody of every age needs to do something more.

Local, national, and international services are desperately calling on us to share ourselves with them, because they know that if each of us does a little, a lot can get done—and growing numbers of these services are recognizing the great value of *young* helping hands.

. . . IS GOOD FOR YOU

No matter how important our involvement may be, many of us often seem to have something better to do with our time and energy. So it may help to remember that, by doing good for others, we can do a lot of good for ourselves.

- If you aren't sure what you want to do with your life, for instance, volunteering can be a way of trying out a variety of different jobs.
- If you *are* sure of what you want to do, you can gather a lot of credentials in the field by working for no pay.
- If you know you're going somewhere but you're not sure where, the credits you earn as a volunteer will make you look better to the people who can help you to get "there."
- If you feel that right now you're only marking time, waiting for "real life" to begin—if the activities enjoyed by the people around you seem at best boring and at worst dangerous—then

you can find a lot of "real life" and a lot of like-minded people right now, by getting involved in a service that means something to *you*.

Are those selfish motives for "doing good"? Maybe so, maybe not—either way, it doesn't matter.

Regardless of what gets you involved in the first place, you'll probably find that you have gained in other ways, as well:

- You will feel good about yourself—simply for doing good.
- You will get to know yourself in ways you can't imagine, simply by putting yourself in situations that are outside of your daily routine.
- You will be able to overcome the sense of powerlessness and frustration that so many of us feel when faced with a world full of troubles.
- You'll find yourself feeling *a part of* life rather than *apart from* it.
- And you can have a lot of fun, spending time doing what *you* choose to, with people who share your interests and outlook.

It's for all these reasons that increasing numbers of high schools are requiring their students to fulfill some sort of community service as part of their education: They know it's good for you, too!

Whatever the motive for volunteering, it's either **good, good, good,** or **better:** *doing* good, *feeling* good, *looking* good, or making something better of *yourself*. You can't beat that—so, what do you do?

TWO

WHAT CAN *I* DO ABOUT IT?

In this "world full of troubles," it's hard to know in which corner to start even though we want to. We tend to feel helpless, or incompetent, or "too busy." We think we are too young (or too old) to be of use. But there is something for each of us, in every situation, at any age, to do.

Some services, like peer counseling or youth hotlines, for instance, can be performed *only* by teens. Through other agencies, young people can teach and tutor, work with the disabled, help the elderly, defend the environment, feed the homeless, rebuild slums, do clerical work that frees professionals from desk jobs, aid in hospitals, channel abundant energy into political and social campaigns . . . you name it.

WHAT YOUR FRIENDS ARE DOING
An estimated ten *million* high school and college students volunteer some of their energy and time at some point throughout

the year. Right now, people your age are working as camp counselors for disabled children, running errands for their older neighbors, writing letters to prisoners and for civic campaigns, guiding tours through museums, finding homes for homeless pets and homeless people, talking on the phone to troubled teens, rebuilding ancient castles in Europe, running computers in research labs, clearing trails in national parks, sewing costumes and hanging lights in local theaters, passing petitions to get out the vote. They are helping to achieve goals that are important to them, living adventures far beyond their normal school-day routine.

And they are having fun—meeting new people in new places, and doing things they enjoy doing. They are raising funds for projects about which they and their communities care with dances, talent shows, bike-a-thons, bake sales, basketball games, street fairs, and mock Olympics. Artists are painting, athletes are playing their sports, musicians are presenting music. Actors act, readers read, singers sing, campers camp, dancers dance, cooks cook, politicians practice politics—all for good causes. You'd be surprised at some of the activities *you* could join.

Doing good doesn't necessarily mean performing noble (and boring) deeds. It can mean doing things—*any* things—at which you want to get better, and feeling good at the same time.

In fact, there are so many possible contributions that you can make as a volunteer, it may be hard to choose.

WHO AM I?

Before you go on to the following chapters about where and how to lend your hand, take a few quiet moments to answer these questions for yourself. They can be a guide to your own most satisfying involvement:

1. What are a few things at which I'm good?
2. What are some things I *enjoy* doing?
3. What would I like to learn to do better?

4. What's an activity I've never done but have always wanted to do?
5. Where do I like to be: indoors? outdoors? close to home? far away?
6. Do I prefer to be: with people? on my own?
7. What kind of people do I like to be with: old? young? like me? different from me?
8. Am I more comfortable with: groups? individuals?
9. What do I want to *gain* from volunteering?
10. What are three problems, in my community or elsewhere, that need solutions?
11. Of *all* the problems that I see or hear about, which ones affect me the most?

As you think about those questions, let's look at some of the possible answers and think about what they mean—for you, and for the kind of contribution you might like to make.

1. What are a few things at which I'm good?

Many people, of *any* age, are unaware of their talents, or they may not value their skills, especially if these abilities don't match up with what the world around them respects as "talents." A woman who is a good cook may downplay that skill because she's always been "just a homebody." A boy who's a good basketball player may not count that skill because he never made the school team. One girl may admit that she's good at getting along with people, but "so what"? High school students who haven't made the honor roll or aren't leaders in a lot of clubs can get the idea that they're not worth much. But that's not true. Each of us is good at something, and those skills become more valuable when we share them with others. What are your skills? Try to name at least three.

2. What are some things I *enjoy* doing?

Too many people still have the attitude that they're "doing good" only if they suffer while they do it—so they don't get involved. Sure, we all want to enjoy life. But volunteering can be a way to do *more*, not less, of what we enjoy. You may think that what you enjoy isn't worth sharing, but that's not true, either. One boy said that all he liked to do was "hang around libraries"—so he found himself taking younger kids to the library after school. A girl who only enjoyed photography began taking pictures at a senior center and was soon teaching photography to the older visitors there. So be real about listing what you enjoy—you'll probably find some way to share that pleasure and make it even more fun.

3. What would I like to learn to do better?

At one time young people could serve as apprentices until they had learned a trade. Today, you can use volunteering as an apprenticeship—as did the would-be writer who was able to show paying editors a portfolio of volunteer writing, or the future politician who learned the campaign ropes before he could even vote. So whether it's typing, teaching, counseling, horseback riding, or whatever you want some more practice at, you can find a way to do it as a volunteer.

4. What's an activity I've never done but have always wanted to do?

A high school student from Maryland spends a summer at the edge of a remote Central American jungle; a midwestern girl sails the Hudson; a young Texan picks grapes in Israel. Faraway places are some people's fantastic fantasies. Maybe they're yours, too. Or maybe you dream of mountain climbing, or seeing the government from the inside, or . . . what? If you pick the right volunteer job, you may be able to try out your dreams. So think of some things you'd *really* like to try.

5. Where do I like to be: indoors? outdoors? close to home? far away?

Some young people seek distant, exotic sites for their volunteer work, or relish a summer in a woodsy work camp—and there are plenty of opportunities for this kind of service. But far away? "Far away" may *not* be your idea of comfort. Many teens find a great deal of satisfaction tutoring in their own school, or being part of a telephone campaign from their own homes. If you aren't the outdoors type, then you're better off helping disabled children by working in an organization's office than counseling at a camp for them—and the children will be better off, too.

6. Do I prefer to be: with people? on my own?

Students in high school clubs and on college campuses flock together for parties or dance-a-thons to raise funds for their charities, and they have a wonderful time. Others enjoy the energy generated by crowds of people who are demonstrating for a cause. At the other end of the scale are the many teens who, in the privacy of their own rooms, write letters to hospitalized or imprisoned people, or in support of the issues that concern them. There's plenty of space in volunteering for both "joiners" and "loners"—so you can be yourself.

7. What kind of people do I like to be with? old? young? like me? different from me?

Two teenagers "share" an elderly neighbor, taking turns visiting her morning and afternoon to help her out. Their friends would rather spend some of their free time after school playing with the kids in a local day-care center. Many young people prefer to join with their friends and classmates on projects, but others look forward to going into different neighborhoods or different countries to be useful. You can help people different from you by joining with people like you, or vice versa: The possibilities are endless, and so are the people who need your help. And you can try out various ways of doing service until you find the way that suits you best.

8. Am I more comfortable with: groups? individuals?

Office work at a voluntary organization, work camps, fundraising events, senior or child-care centers—these are a few "group" activities that need doing. Tutoring, being a friendly visitor in a hospital, "adopting" a disabled neighbor—these are some one-on-one possibilities. And in between? Canvassing for political or social campaigns, running a sales or information desk at a museum or the like—you name it. You can do it.

9. What do I want to *gain* from volunteering?

Chapter 1 showed you how volunteering could be good for *you*. So what do you want from it: An adventure? Career help? A shiny star on your record? Pure satisfaction for your soul? Power over a seemingly overwhelming problem? The pleasure of spending time with people who share your interests? Fun? You can get any or all of those benefits from volunteering—so don't be timid about saying "I want. . . ."

10. What are three problems, in my community or elsewhere, that need solutions?

This one is really up to you. And if you can't find three, you're not looking!

11. Of *all* the problems that I see or hear about, which ones affect me the most?

In the list of questions, this one may be the most important for the success of your volunteering experiences. Here's why.

The dictionary defines "charity" as "The kindly and *sympathetic* disposition to aid the needy or suffering." That word, "sympathetic," is important because it means "feeling with," and it's vital for both your satisfaction and your usefulness as a volunteer that you feel *with* the people or situation you choose to help.

The word "charity" isn't used too much today: It has taken on the meaning of something we *ought* to do if we are good people, a duty that the fortunates ("us") have toward the unfortunates ("them"). The word "volunteering," on the other hand, has to do with "being willing," with *wanting* to help. And it's important to know what you really *want* to do, since doing your "duty" for "them" will soon become tiresome.

So, of all the needs close to home or far away, which do you most feel with—and why? A well-done magazine article or television documentary may inspire you briefly—but is it a cause you care enough about to be willing to help? Your friends may all be lining up to feed the homeless, but is that really for you? Only you can decide.

Perhaps a friend was killed on the road, and you want to do something about drunk driving. Maybe your grandfather was your favorite person, and working with old people helps you to remember him. Your best times may have been hiking in the woods, and you feel strongly about protecting the wilderness so that you and others can continue to enjoy that experience.

We each have our own reasons for the volunteering we do—reasons that might not make sense to others, but are important to us. Simply by thinking about them, we've already begun to gain some of the personal benefits of volunteering: We're getting to know ourselves better!

Now go back to the list on page 8 and think over the questions with honesty and care before going on to the suggestions in the following section.

As you think about them, you may quickly learn something new about yourself. You may admit to skills you didn't think you had. You may find that activities you thought you enjoyed were really only being done out of habit. Some volunteers want to do what they always do, but in a different setting. Others choose some activity totally outside of their normal routine.

A writer seeking volunteer work wanted to be actively involved with people, because her work forced her to spend a lot of time alone. Unfortunately, most of the agencies she contacted wanted only to use her writing skills, and they preferred that she write at home, alone! You'll find tips in a later chapter about how best to fit your needs and interests into the demands of voluntary organizations.

But first, you'll need to select from among the *many* possibilities. In order to do the most good for others and for yourself, you'll want to carefully choose the activities to which you lend your hand.

That is what the remaining chapters in this book will help you to do.

PART
TWO

WHERE TO
VOLUNTEER

THREE

WHO NEEDS HELP; WHAT THEY DO; HOW TO FIND THEM

"I'd like to help out—really I would. But there's no way I can do anything that really interests me. Besides—I'm just a kid. No place that matters is going to want *my* help."

Have you ever heard somebody say something like that? Have you ever heard *yourself* say it? Well, guess what? You're wrong, and the next 135 pages will prove it.

HOW TO USE THIS SECTION
To help you decide where best to lend your hand, in this section are detailed descriptions of over one hundred organizations devoted to one type of volunteer work or another. Along with them are additional ideas for similar service: other places where you might look; things that other young people have done; efforts that you might undertake on your own or with your friends.

The suggestions are grouped into broad categories according to the kinds of involvement that most people seek. If you have answered the questions on page 8, you should be able to find quickly the categories best suited to your interests. (On the other hand, if those answers showed you that you're looking for something *not* included within these topics, turn to "More Ways to Lend Your Hand," beginning on page 140.)

The lists are categorized by the *content* of the work the groups do—involvement that focuses (in alphabetical order) on:

> Animals
> Arts and Culture
> Children
> Civil Rights and Civic Issues
> Diseases and Disabilities
> Drugs and Alcohol
> The Elderly
> Hunger and Homelessness
> Illiteracy
> International Cooperation
> Nature and the Environment
> Politics and Government
> Prisoners
> Teenagers
> Plus—Social-Service Organizations (multipurpose associations that deal with a variety of issues)

Most of the organizations listed here are national or international, with local or regional centers. Some serve only a limited area, but can provide ideas or references for you if you don't live near them. And there are *lots* of specific ideas for finding agencies and groups that serve your local community.

Each entry describes the organization, lists its address and phone number, and summarizes its purpose, need for volunteers, and the type of work available. For each group, a statement of the benefits that volunteering for that project can bring is also included. (Along with these detailed listings are the names of additional organizations that might be worth investigating or that can serve as a resource, though they provided no special information when contacted for this book.)

With this information, you'll be able to find not only a cause that matters to you, but activities that fit the skills, needs, and interests you pinpointed in the questionnaire on page 8.

If you already have a specific organization in mind, check the names in the alphabetical listing at the back of the book.

But—if you still think there's "nothing to do," just flip through the next 133 pages and browse a bit. You may be surprised by the great variety of volunteer activities listed here—and you may be even more surprised to learn that these are only a small fraction of the literally tens of thousands of national, regional, and local organizations that are working together toward the solution of problems that some people think are "impossible" to deal with. (And how to find those thousands of others? See "Check It Out," beginning on page 149.)

All of the groups listed here have at least two things in common: They all need help, and they are all looking for *you*.

So start looking, get in touch, and get involved!

ANIMALS

Animals come in all shapes and sizes—and with all kinds of needs. Pets can be loving and loyal; they accept our love and need a lot of it. They and other domesticated animals are totally dependent on humans for their care, safety, and comfort. Wild animals, too, need human help if they are to survive.

If you love animals, you may just want to be with them and share the pleasure they can give; you may want to explore a career related to animals; or you may agree with animal-rights activists that the way we treat animals is a reflection of the way we feel about ourselves as humans. Whatever your reasons, you have a variety of ways to get involved with animals as a volunteer.

In addition to joining the activities of the groups listed here, teenagers work as volunteers at their local veterinarian's office or animal shelter. (But remember, while there's fun and pleasure in that work, there also may be the pain of dealing with sickness and death.)

Research has shown that animals can provide a unique kind of therapy to the sick or lonely, so young people also share their own love of animals with others by taking pets (their own or a shelter's) to hospitals, nursing homes, or day-care centers. In those ways, you can combine a concern for children, the elderly, or sick or disabled people with your interest in animals.

The following entries will give you an idea of the scope of volunteer possibilities in this area.

AMERICAN SOCIETY
FOR THE PREVENTION
OF CRUELTY TO ANIMALS
(ASPCA)
441 East 92nd Street, New York, NY 10128
(212) 876-7700

America's first humane society, committed to protecting animals locally, statewide, and nationally.

Activities: Provides direct care, rescue, and protection to animals in New York state and city; nationwide, actively supports legislation against cruelty to animals; sponsors animal-protection education; and serves as a clearinghouse for other animal-welfare organizations. Special project: Pet-Assisted Therapy Program, in which volunteers take animals to nursing homes, hospitals, and other institutions to lift patient morale.

Volunteer Opportunities: Well-organized volunteer network for administrative, animal-care, and public-information duties at New York office; those interested in this work in other areas can distribute information, or use the central office as an ideas' resource for local activities.

Contact: National headquarters.

> **"By encouraging the humane treatment of animals, the Society promotes the noblest instincts of mankind and seeks to enhance the quality of all life."**

FRIENDS OF ANIMALS
1 Pine Street, Neptune, NJ 07753
(201) 922–2600

A national nonprofit membership organization that works to reduce and eliminate the suffering of animals in order "to achieve
a humane ethic in humanity's relationship with the nonhumans
of this earth."

Activities: Provides low-cost breeding-control services for animals in communities throughout the country to reduce the numbers of unwanted pets; works to protect wildlife and to prevent
and eliminate laboratory experimentation with animals; produces educational materials; and raises funds for these activities.

Volunteer Opportunities: Participate in all activities at a local
level, including organizing community programs where they don't
yet exist. Volunteers receive information and support material
from the national office.

Contact: National headquarters.

> **"More than 14 million unwanted cats and
> dogs are killed in pounds and shelters each
> year. Volunteers provide their communi-
> ties with a solution to this problem."**

THE HUMANE SOCIETY
OF THE UNITED STATES
2100 L Street, NW, Washington, DC 20037
(202) 452–1100

The nation's largest animal-welfare organization, with 500,000 volunteers who work with local agencies to improve the lives of pets, laboratory animals, wildlife, and farm animals.
Activities: Investigates, educates, and supports legislation toward prevention of cruelty to animals. Trains animal-control and animal-welfare workers in humane treatment.
Volunteer Opportunities: Help in all activities of national and regional offices; work in local shelters that follow Society guidelines.
Contact: National headquarters for location of regional offices and local groups.

> **"The work of preventing abuse and suffering to animals is not only an obligation toward other creatures; it is also a stage in the development of mankind toward that quality of being we call human."**

PEOPLE FOR THE ETHICAL
TREATMENT OF ANIMALS (PETA)
P.O. Box 42516, Washington, DC 20015
(202) 726-0156

An educational and activist group opposed to all forms of "speciesism," animal oppression and exploitation by humans, including inhumane trapping, laboratory experiments, and factory farming.

Activities: Members hold regular workshops; stage media events to draw attention to animal abuse; distribute educational materials; maintain letterwriting and phone campaigns; demonstrate against institutions that abuse animals.

Volunteer Opportunities: Participate as a member in all activities on a local level with support from national organization; or use pamphlets from national headquarters to follow their suggestions on your own about "how to prevent animal suffering in your daily life."

Contact: National headquarters for location of nearest affiliate.

> **"If we want to help animals, the most important place to start is with our own lifestyles, learning to live without cruelty."**

OTHER RESOURCES

To find a local animal-protection agency that follows humane practices, contact:

AMERICAN HUMANE ASSOCIATION
Animal Protection Division
P.O. Box 1266
Denver, CO 80201
(303) 695–0811

This is a national organization of agencies and individuals committed to protecting animals (and children) from neglect, cruelty, abuse, and exploitation.

If you want to learn to care for animals, find the nearest 4-H club or office of the Extension Service of the U.S. Department of Agriculture.

Interested in a specific type or breed of animal? Look in the *Encyclopedia of Associations* (see page 149) for organizations devoted to it.

See also: "Nature and the Environment" entries (pages 94–107).

ARTS AND CULTURE

Music, theater, dance, writing, painting, sculpture—these are not the exclusive provinces of big-city professionals, or even of adults. Although you may be one of the many young people who feel a strong commitment to the arts, you may not believe that you have any right to share your talent until you have developed it further. On the other hand, like Richard, the musician offered as an example at the opening of this book, you may not want to do anything *but* your art.

Volunteering offers many ways to learn, practice, and share the art you love—whether you live in a major cultural center or not. In fact, arts facilities in smaller communities are likely to be the ones in most need of enthusiastic unpaid help.

Teenagers across the country work in **galleries and museums** as guides, information aides, clerks, and curators' assistants. They help local **theaters** with costumes, sets, lights, and front-of-house duties. Dancers and musicians support their local **performance groups,** from raising funds and distributing publicity through joining in the performances. **Writers** work for community papers, or produce newsletters and brochures for volunteer groups. And while these young people are "doing good," they stay close to their art and learn firsthand what goes on behind the scenes.

Even if you have a very special dream shared by nobody you know, you can find a way to explore that unique fascination by volunteering. Historical **archaeologists** are digging in the most unexpected places around the country, and are always looking for help. Public **radio and television** stations need help—with fundraising, and often with other tasks that can get you close to the action. Or see what you can do for a campus station that students at your local college operate. **Architects,** especially in smaller firms, are usually happy to have unpaid, interested assistance, and the same is true for **photographers**—look them up in the phone book and ask. **History** buffs can help research the past of their community or county, and **crafts** enthusiasts can seek out regional craftspeople to learn traditional work.

If you're interested in culture in general, don't overlook the vibrant spectrum of **ethnic arts,** a cultural source that enriches not only one particular heritage, but that of the community as a whole. Native Americans, Hispanics, Blacks, and nationality groups from Afghanis through Zambians all work to keep their cultures alive—and they all are especially eager to find young people who want to participate and pass along their heritages to others. If you find no active promotion of the arts of *your* ethnic group in your area, you can probably get something going just by showing your interest.

And, no matter who you are or where you live, you can *share your talent.* Young people, individually or in groups, sing, dance, and play their music at centers for the old, the young, or the ill. They escort groups to concerts, plays, and museums. And they teach their arts to others: You can help a deprived or disabled child learn to take a photograph or make music; you can show an old or ill adult how to paint or sculpt, or help a hospital patient to write a letter or a poem; you can bring a group to life by organizing it into a theatrical company. There's no better way to learn than to teach—and no better way to realize how skilled you already are than to help someone else develop that skill.

Maybe, in addition to your art, there's a cause about which you really care that's listed in one of the other sections. You can *combine your interests* by performing or putting on shows to attract attention or raise funds for any volunteer group, or you can design posters, banners, and the like. You'll not only be making an important contribution, but you'll discover that you do, indeed, have a talent that other people value.

So, with your art in mind, decide in which of the many possible settings you'd like to share it. Then look through the entries in the other sections here, check the phone book, or explore your community for groups that can make good use of your talent— and you.

OTHER RESOURCES

Although research indicates that no nationwide organization exists whose mission is to inform or coordinate volunteers in the arts, you can find an outlet for your interest by going directly to the arts institutions that appeal to you, or by checking your areas of interest in *The Encyclopedia of Associations*. Or, call:

the nearest **Chamber of Commerce**
city, county, or state **Arts Councils**
or **Commissions on Culture**
your **library.**

If you have no success with those efforts, try:

THE CENTER FOR ARTS INFORMATION
625 Broadway
New York, NY 10012
(212) 977–2544

Although the primary purpose of these organizations is not to assist the general public, their staffs can help you to locate an arts organization in your area if you're really stuck.

The following agency has access to experts in every area of the arts who may be able to refer you to an organization of interest. Ask for the Public Information Office.

NATIONAL ENDOWMENT FOR THE ARTS
1100 Pennsylvania Avenue, NW
Washington, DC 20004
(202) 682–5400

CHILDREN

No matter what your age, a younger child looks up to you—and that admiration can provide a wonderful feeling. That's probably why so many volunteers are interested in working with children. But if you're someone who's had it up to here with babysitting or watching out for younger siblings, you'll be happy to learn that "working with children" doesn't have to mean child *care*.

Teenagers are coaching teams of disabled or retarded youngsters, helping young refugees learn English, keeping in touch with lonely kids at home by themselves, playing with little ones in after-school centers and hospital nurseries, teaching safety skills to elementary-school classes: From Sunday schools to skating rinks, they're giving a little to kids, and getting a lot back.

Whatever it is you love to do—gardening or sports, music or computers—you'll find it even more rewarding when you share it with a child. It's tough being a kid today. Even those who are healthy may be lonely or bored if they're home on their own; or they may be frightened by the threatening environment they either live in or hear about daily. For those who are ill, or disabled, or homeless, the days are even harder—and you can make a difference in their lives, simply by doing with them things that you like to do yourself.

So if you enjoy children, contact local schools, hospitals, religious organizations, or child-protection agencies to see what you can do for the kids in your community. Or, lend your hand to activities for children sponsored by service groups like Key Club or Scouts.

Many national and international organizations exist to aid children on a broader scale than individuals or entire communities are able to. Some of those groups are listed on the following pages. As these entries indicate, you can help directly to solve a variety of the problems children face, or you can help indirectly, by getting together to raise funds to support some urgent causes. Even if you *have* had it up to here with child care, you can still act on your very real concern for children.

ACTION FOR CHILDREN'S
TELEVISION (ACT)

20 University Road, Cambridge, MA 02138
(617) 876-6620

A national nonprofit consumer-advocacy organization that works
to encourage diversity in children's television and to eliminate
commercial abuses targeted to young viewers.

Activities: Initiates legal reform and promotes public awareness
of issues relating to children's television through public education campaigns, awards, publications, and conferences.

Volunteer Opportunities: Join membership of 20,000 who support goals through activities in their communities; also, in internship program, volunteers (primarily but not exclusively college
students) work at headquarters office in all aspects of projects.

Contact: National headquarters.

> **"Children—and through them, society—
> can be helped or harmed by television. ACT
> works toward developing the beneficial as-
> pects of television. ACT volunteers learn
> how an advocacy group works to change
> the way that institutions deal with the
> public interest."**

CHILD FIND, INC.
P.O. Box 277, New Paltz, NY 12561
1–800–I–AM–LOST

A private nonprofit national organization dedicated solely to child safety and the task of registering and locating missing children. Since its founding in 1980, it has helped to find over 1,600 missing children.

Activities: Locates missing children through a national network; counsels families of lost children; mediates child-custody disputes; distributes directory of missing children and child-safety materials.

Volunteer Opportunities: Through "Friends of Child Find" affiliates, work with children and adults on child safety and locating projects within individual communities.

Contact: National headquarters for location of nearest affiliate.

> **"For every missing child there are parents, relatives, friends, and neighbors who are suffering the greatest loss a person can endure. Child Find gives hope to those whose search continues."**

FOSTER PARENTS PLAN
Department 113
155 Plan Way, Warwick, RI 02886
1-800-556-7918, extension 212

A private nonprofit international child-sponsorship and development organization working to improve the quality of life for children in Asia, Africa, and Central and South America.

Activities: Connects Americans with individual needy children overseas as a way of providing for both immediate urgent needs and developing long-term solutions to the needy community's problems. Each Foster Parent contributes $22 per year and exchanges photographs and letters with their Foster children overseas.

Volunteer Opportunities: Become a Foster Parent on your own or with your family or a group, by making a small donation. You will be put in touch with a needy child. Volunteers are also needed to help in the seventy Volunteer Support Groups throughout the country with their educational, fundraising, and other activities.

Contact: National headquarters.

> **"Your love can change a lifetime. You participate in helping a needy child and family in a country overseas while learning something about the social and cultural conditions in which they live."**

MAIL FOR TOTS
25 New Charndon Street, P.O. Box 8699
Boston, MA 02114

Collects and distributes lists of children (and needy adults) who are chronically ill, hospitalized, or otherwise isolated, and who appreciate receiving letters, cards, and other mail.

Activities: Assigns a child to a volunteer for correspondence; circulates lists and publicizes efforts to become pen pals with the sick and lonely.

Volunteer Activities: Become a correspondent.

Contact: National headquarters.

> **"This is an easy task that takes little time and can be done at long distance, yet the mail is greatly appreciated."**

MAKE-A-WISH FOUNDATION
OF AMERICA

4601 16th Street, Suite 205
Phoenix, AZ 85016
(602) 234–0960

A national nonprofit corporation whose purpose is to grant the favorite wish of terminally ill children. Several thousand wishes have been granted since the group's founding in 1980; many are costly.

Activities: Arranges, through a network of regional chapters and medical personnel, to grant a wish of almost any variety to a terminally ill child up to age eighteen, anywhere in the world; raises funds to support work.

Volunteer Opportunities: Be available to local chapter to assist in wish-granting; help to raise funds.

Contact: National headquarters, or see phone book for local chapter.

> **"The Foundation counts its accomplishments in the smiling faces of the children whose wishes have been granted."**

SAVE THE CHILDREN
FEDERATION, INC.
54 Wilton Road, Westport, CT 06880
(203) 226–7272

A national organization that for over fifty years has sponsored community-based integrated self-help programs in underdeveloped areas throughout the United States and the world.

Activities: Researchers and field staff select areas of great need and gain the cooperation of community members and government agencies to attack immediate crises created by disease, hunger, or devastation and aid the community in developing long-term solutions to their social, economic, and educational problems.

Volunteer Opportunities: Organize fun fundraising events; sponsor a needy child; spread information about the organization.

Contact: National headquarters for location of nearest chapter.

> **"Your time and energy can help communities give their children a chance."**

THE U.S. COMMITTEE FOR UNICEF
331 East 38th Street, New York, NY 10016
(212) 686–5522

One of 34 national committees around the world whose purpose is to raise funds for projects in the 118 developing countries assisted by UNICEF (The United Nations Children's Fund), and to educate the American public about the needs of children in the developing world.

Activities: Raises funds through events, sale of cards, and "trick-or-treating"; spreads information in schools and communities about UNICEF's work and the condition of the children it helps.

Volunteer Opportunities: Organize a fundraising event; organize sale of greeting cards, or trick-or-treating—or do it on your own; represent UNICEF at fairs, meetings, and other public gatherings.

Contact: National headquarters, or these regional offices:

West:
1875 Century Park East
Los Angeles CA 90067
(213) 555–1191

Midwest:
540 N. Michigan Avenue
Chicago, IL 60611
(312) 670–2379

Central:
1360 Post Oak Boulevard
Houston, TX 77056
(713) 963–9390

Southeast:
3384 Peachtree Road NE
Atlanta, GA 30326
(404) 233–9429

> **"UNICEF works toward guaranteeing a future for every child. By volunteering, you can make a positive difference for the world's children."**

OTHER RESOURCES

Child Welfare Bureau
or city, county, or state **Department of Social Services**

THE AMERICAN ASSOCIATION
FOR PROTECTING CHILDREN
P.O. Box 1266
Denver, CO 80201
(303) 695–0811

See also: "Diseases and Disabilities" entries (pages 51–64).

CIVIL RIGHTS AND CIVIC ISSUES

Is there one issue you *really* care about—one item that, when you hear about it on the news, either makes your blood simmer with rage or brings a lump of emotion to your throat? This is the kind of issue with which the groups listed in this section deal: controversial topics that affect people where they *believe*.

No one can tell you which side to take, or which group among all of them, including the few listed here, is most deserving of your attention—that's part of *your* civil rights, after all. But you should be told that teens who believe in these and many other local, national, and international causes are actively working for them.

They are getting signatures on petitions, walking in demonstrations, handing out literature, gathering data for research projects, meeting with their elected officials and representatives, making phone calls, writing letters, and working on the projects and toward the goals of organizations like the ones listed here.

AMERICAN CIVIL LIBERTIES UNION (ACLU)

132 West 43rd Street, New York, NY 10036
(212) 944–9800

National nonpartisan organization whose sole purpose is to protect Americans' rights to freedom of expression, belief, and association, to fairness, privacy, and equal treatment before the law, and to defend them from the "tyranny of the majority."

Activities: Through national offices and nationwide network of affiliates and chapters, litigates, educates, and supports legislation to protect and defend constitutionally guaranteed civil liberties.

Volunteer Opportunities: Local and state groups need nonprofessional volunteers to help with mail and phone campaigns, educational and promotional efforts, and fundraising activities.

Contact: National headquarters for location of nearest affiliate.

> **"So long as we have enough people in this country willing to fight for their rights, we'll be called a democracy."**

AMERICAN INDIAN HERITAGE FOUNDATION

6051 Arlington Boulevard
Falls Church, VA 22044
(703) 237-7500

A nonprofit nonpartisan service organization with the goal of encouraging more Americans to become involved in improving the lives of Native Americans.

Activities: Educates non-Indians in cultures and needs of Native Americans; educates and encourages Indian achievement; distributes emergency supplies of food and clothing to tribal people in need; develops markets for Indian handicrafts; sponsors several special events each year, including American Indian Heritage Week and July 4 Pow-Wow.

Volunteer Opportunities: Help with clerical and other activities in offices; work short-term on special events; provide services within Indian communities and reservations nationwide.

Contact: National headquarters.

> **"The foundation is reaching out to meet the physical and spiritual needs of Indians across the country. Several thousand caring individuals, like you and me, are contributing regularly to this important work."**

CONGRESS OF RACIAL EQUALITY
(CORE)

1457 Flatbush Avenue, Brooklyn, NY 11210
(718) 434–3580

National civil- and human-rights organization working toward the goal of true equality for all people throughout the world.
Activities: Works locally, nationally, and internationally to eliminate discrimination and provide services in a variety of areas, including community development, substance abuse, prison reform, unemployment, housing, education, and voter registration.
Volunteer Opportunities: Participate at a local level in all activities; also participate as a community worker in Summer Youth Program.
Contact: National headquarters.

> **"Membership in CORE is open to anyone who believes that all people are created equal and is willing to work toward the goal of equality."**

NATIONAL COALITION TO BAN HANDGUNS

100 Maryland Avenue, NE
Washington, DC 20002
(202) 544-7190

A coalition of national organizations united to combat the problem of handgun violence through the orderly elimination of all handguns from U.S. society.

Activities: Lobbies; provides public education, research, and legal assistance on national, state, and local levels.

Volunteer Opportunities: Help in Washington office; join activities of local groups; or send for pamphlet containing facts and suggested activities.

Contact: National headquarters.

> **"There is an epidemic of deaths and injuries among children and youth due to one source—the handgun."**

NATIONAL GAY & LESBIAN TASK FORCE

1517 U Street, NW, Washington, DC 20009
(202) 332–6483

Civil-rights-advocacy organization that works to achieve freedom from discrimination for gay men and lesbians.
Activities: Lobbies; helps with community organizing and public education campaigns; and provides information and other resources to groups throughout the country.
Volunteer Opportunities: A variety of tasks in Washington office; information resource about local and regional groups.
Contact: National headquarters.

"Volunteers enable the Task Force to be active on all fronts at all times."

NATIONAL ORGANIZATION FOR WOMEN, INC. (NOW)
1401 New York Avenue, NW
Washington, DC 20005
(202) 347–2279

Organization of 700 chapters nationwide dedicated to bringing women into full participation in the mainstream of American society.

Activities: Publicizes, promotes, and actively supports legislation and other efforts toward political, economic, and personal rights for women.

Volunteer Opportunities: Local chapters need help with all activities, from office work through campaigns and special events; unpaid interns work (by application) in national office and locations around country.

Contact: National headquarters, or see phone book for local chapter.

> **"There *is* something you can do to make equality a reality for your sister, your mother, your daughter, yourself—now."**

NATIONAL RIFLE ASSOCIATION
1600 Rhode Island Avenue, NW
Washington, DC 20036
(202) 828-6000

Membership organization of gun owners and hunters.
Activities: Through 12,000 local groups, trains in firearm use; promotes firearm safety and wildlife conservation; sponsors competitions; lobbies extensively on firearm issues.
Volunteer Opportunities: As a member, participate in all activities; or help with lobbying and educational efforts.
Contact: National headquarters for location of nearest chapter.

"Guns don't kill; people do."

NATIONAL YOUTH PRO-LIFE COALITION
Jackson Avenue
Hastings-on-Hudson, NY 10706
(914) 478–0103

A coordinating organization for nonpartisan nonsectarian local and regional high school and college pro-life groups, working toward the development of a consistent attitude toward the value and dignity of human life.

Activities: Groups seek the creation and implementation of positive nonviolent solutions to human problems, including abortion, euthanasia, fetal experimentation, and social treatment of prisoners and the elderly; national office works to organize local groups, sponsors educational and promotional events, and provides leadership training for local groups.

Volunteer Opportunities: Clerical and public contact work at national office; or join or form a local group.

Contact: National headquarters for location of nearest chapter.

"Human life is a continuum from conception until natural death; there is no such thing as the human life not worth living."

OPERATION PUSH, INC.
930 East 50th Street, Chicago, IL 60615
(312) FREEDOM

*P*eople *U*nited to *S*erve *H*umanity, founded by Rev. Jesse Jackson to continue the war against political injustice, poverty, unemployment, drugs, and hunger, and for human and civil rights.
Activities: Acts and educates to promote Black businesses; improves local public education and motivates students; mobilizes voter registration, primarily in Black and Hispanic communities; and supports social programs to strengthen families and combat poverty and hunger.
Volunteer Opportunities: Participate in all activities through state and local chapters.
Contact: National headquarters for location of nearest chapter.

"Nobody will save us for us. But us."

PEOPLE FOR THE AMERICAN WAY
1424 16th Street, NW, Washington, DC 20036
(202) 462–4777

A national nonpartisan public-interest organization dedicated to promoting constitutional liberties.

Activities: Educational, promotional, research, and activism for support of: religious liberty and pluralism; freedom to learn and excellence in education; independence of the judiciary; and access to information and the freedom to know.

Volunteer Opportunities: In "grassroots program" to monitor events in local communities and organize when needed to protect liberties. Volunteers organized at local level through regional field coordinators.

Contact: National headquarters for location of nearest chapter.

> **"Our volunteers proudly stand up for our principles and theirs: basic democratic values like pluralism, tolerance, diversity, and freedom of speech and religion."**

PLANNED PARENTHOOD
810 Seventh Avenue, New York, NY 10019
(212) 541–7800

The nation's oldest and largest voluntary family-planning agency, dedicated to the principle that every individual has the fundamental right to make an independent decision about having children.

Activities: Nearly 200 agencies in 45 states provide or supervise medical services and counseling; offer educational programs for community groups, schools, and professionals; work with other groups to provide access to planning and health services, and to promote well-being of individuals, families, and communities; support public education and legislative campaigns; raise funds for activities and services.

Volunteer Opportunities: Vary by area; each group has its own needs.

Contact: National headquarters, or see phone book for local chapter.

> **"Each year, 3 million Americans, many with low incomes, receive the highest quality medical, educational, or counseling services from Planned Parenthood's centers."**

OTHER RESOURCES

These groups, which responded to research requests for this book, are only a few of the many rights-related organizations that exist to reflect every shade of opinion. If none here inspires you, check the reference books listed on page 149. You'll find that many, but by no means all, of the others focus on religious beliefs or ethnic issues with which you may feel kinship. Whether it's the Anti-Defamation League, the NAACP, the League of Latin Americans, or whatever, look for ones that fire you up. They'll be more than glad to add another worker for their cause, and your contribution will provide you with some invaluable experience.

See also: "Hunger and Homelessness" (pages 73–78); "Illiteracy" (pages 79–82); "International Cooperation" (pages 83–93); "Nature and the Environment" (pages 94–107); "Politics and Government"(pages 108–112);and"Prisoners"(pages 113–116) entries for groups that deal with other *social* issues.

DISEASES AND DISABILITIES

A high school student required to perform community service couldn't decide on a satisfying project until the school's volunteer coordinator mentioned physical disabilities. This suggestion appealed to her. "My mother is blind," she said, and went to work for a local agency serving the blind.

You, too, may have a special interest in a particular kind of disease or disability, because of family or personal experience. Working with an organization devoted to curing or coping with that condition is a good way not only to help solve the problem, but also to gain knowledge and a greater understanding of your own feelings about it.

Personal experience is not a requirement, however, for volunteer work with any of the groups listed here, or with similar organizations. They may simply perform services that you respect, or work toward goals that you share. You can also help sick people by volunteering at your local hospital, but unless you want to, it's not necessary to deal *directly* with the diseases or disabling conditions. Many people have a hard time confronting illness or disability, but like them, you'll find plenty of ways to support these and other groups on both a short- and long-term basis by joining with others in fundraising or public-awareness events, for instance, or by using your special talents to help them achieve their goals.

Also, don't assume that diseases have to be depressing. One high school junior was prepared to feel really saddened by her prospective "good-deed" work with handicapped children—but after her first day as a camp counselor, she realized that the children's eagerness and enthusiasm had filled her with energy.

As with every kind of volunteer activity, you can count on getting at least as much as you give when you get involved with organizations like those listed in this section.

AMERICAN HEART ASSOCIATION (AHA)

7320 Greenville Avenue, Dallas, TX 75231
(214) 373–6300

The largest national voluntary health agency in the United States dedicated to the reduction, through prevention and treatment, of early death and disability from cardiovascular diseases and stroke—the nation's leading killers that cause almost half of annual deaths.

Activities: Sponsors and funds research and educational and community-service programs.

Volunteer Opportunities: In addition to professionals in medicine and other fields, needs nonprofessionals of all ages to help raise funds and distribute information door to door and through organizing or participating in special events. Has "Schoolsite" program to spread knowledge and practice of heart-saving lifestyles; students can encourage and support these activities. Uses over two million volunteers, organized through committees on state and local levels.

Contact: AHA organizations in all states and Puerto Rico; branches in over 3,000 communities. See phone book for local chapter.

> **"As long as almost a million Americans continue to lose their lives every year due to cardiovascular disease, Americans should support research and education on it. AHA volunteers can gain experience and develop talents while being involved in rewarding social activities."**

AMERICAN LUNG ASSOCIATION (ALA)

1740 Broadway, New York, NY 10019
(212) 315–8700

Originally founded to combat tuberculosis, the ALA is the oldest national voluntary organization; its purpose now is to control and prevent all lung diseases and some of their causes; efforts to eliminate smoking are its top priority.

Activities: Promotes and funds research and educational and community-service programs, supported by donations to "Easter Seals" and other contributions.

Volunteer Opportunities: Needs nonprofessional help in fund drives and in distribution of educational materials; special interest in reaching young people on dangers of smoking.

Contact: Associations in all states and most large cities. See phone book for local chapter.

> **"Once, tuberculosis was an epidemic; today it is not. But today more than 47 million men, women and children suffer from chronic lung disease caused mainly by smoking and other environmental factors—and the work of the ALA is far from over."**

ARTHRITIS FOUNDATION
1314 Spring Street, NW, Atlanta, GA 30309
(404) 872–7100

A national organization that funds and supports scientific research about arthritis, "the nation's number one crippling disease," and works to provide improved health services to victims of arthritis.

Activities: Sponsors fundraising for medical research; public education; provision of information and treatment referrals to arthritis victims.

Volunteer Activities: Keeping in mind that many arthritis sufferers are children and young people, teens can help with educational efforts and with office work that provides information to victims and their families. Requires no special training.

Contact: National headquarters for location of nearest chapter.

> **"Arthritis cripples and disables over 31 million Americans, including hundreds of thousands of children and young people. Each year the disease claims 1 million new victims, and there is no cure. Everyone has some special talent or skill, and we can put your experience to work."**

CANCER CARE, INC. and
THE NATIONAL CANCER CARE
FOUNDATION, INC.

1180 Avenue of the Americas
New York, NY 10036
(212) 221–3300

A nonprofit agency, separate from other cancer-related organizations, founded to help cancer patients, their friends, and families to cope with the impact of cancer.

Activities: Provides free psychological counseling, practical guidance, and financial support to cancer patients and their families at all stages of the disease, as well as education and training for health-care professionals.

Volunteer Opportunities: Laypeople of any age can serve as "Friendly Visitors" to homebound cancer patients, once an interview has determined that they are suitable for the work. Volunteers participate in a training program and regular support-group meetings. This activity can be stressful, but also most rewarding—and many cancer patients are young people especially in need of encouragement.

Contact: Cancer Care, Inc. serves clients only in the greater New York/New Jersey and Los Angeles metropolitan areas. If you are interested in this kind of work but live elsewhere, the group's headquarters may be able to offer you alternative suggestions.

> **"Until the cure, we offer the care: Our volunteers, in addition to gaining new skills in a supportive environment, receive the satisfaction of knowing they are part of a movement to make ours a responsive, caring society."**

MARCH OF DIMES BIRTH DEFECTS FOUNDATION
1275 Mamaroneck Avenue
White Plains, NY 10605
(914) 428–7100

National organization devoted to preventing birth defects—more than 3,000 disorders that strike over 250,000 babies in the United States each year.

Activities: Sponsors research, public education, and medical services, and raises funds to support these projects.

Volunteer Opportunities: In all areas, but especially in fundraising, through events such as the annual WalkAmerica drive. Many local and regional chapters have special student-volunteer programs for junior high and high school students.

Contact: National headquarters for local chapter.

> **"Students are the leaders of WalkAmerica and have an important role in the fight against birth defects."**

MUSCULAR DYSTROPHY ASSOCIATION (MDA)

810 Seventh Avenue, New York, NY 10019
(212) 586–0808

A voluntary national health agency working to defeat forty neuromuscular diseases—which create in children, teens, and older people a progressive inability to control body movements—through a worldwide research program, comprehensive patient and community services, and broad professional and public-health education.

Activities: Funds and supports research into the causes and treatments of these diseases; provides patient and community services to aid in coping, professional and public education programs, and a summer camping program throughout the country.

Volunteer Opportunities: Uses two million volunteers of all ages annually in fundraising through the organization of events or participation in the annual telethon run by chairman Jerry Lewis, and in the distribution of educational materials. It also needs counselors—especially high school and college students—for its seventy-two special summer camps for children.

Contact: National headquarters, or see phone book for local chapter.

> **"There are no incurable diseases, only diseases for which no treatments have yet been found. MDA relies on volunteers to help find ways to find a cure and to help victims until the cure can be found."**

NATIONAL AIDS NETWORK
1012 14th Street, NW
Washington, DC 20005
(202) 347–0390

A national central clearinghouse for information on Acquired Immune Deficiency Syndrome (AIDS) and on organizations working on various aspects of the disease.

Activities: Provides information and education about AIDS to people with the disease and those who work with them.

Volunteer Opportunities: None for NAN itself, but anyone interested in helping people with AIDS can get suggestions and referrals through the network.

Contact: National headquarters.

> **"There was a time when people concerned with AIDS had few places to turn. Today, for better or for worse, the options are many."**

NATIONAL EASTER SEAL SOCIETY
2023 West Ogden Avenue, Chicago, IL 60612
(312) 243–8400

A nationwide network of state and local societies whose cooperative efforts provide services for more than one million people a year with physical and mental disabilities caused by a wide variety of conditions. Its goal is "to put the ability in disability."

Activities: Helps people with disabilities to solve physical, emotional, financial, legal, medical, social, and employment problems; aids communities in developing services and facilities for people with disabilities within a climate of acceptance; promotes and sponsors research that directly aids people with disabilities.

Volunteer Opportunities: All-encompassing, from answering telethon phone calls and organizing events through sewing special clothing or developing a relationship with an individual disabled person. Each community has different specific needs, but every society offers chances for a variety of work, either as an individual or through service organizations.

Contact: National headquarters, or see phone book for local chapter.

> **"People who volunteer for Easter Seals provide persons with disabilities opportunities to reach their full potential in their communities."**

NATIONAL FEDERATION
OF THE BLIND
1800 Johnson Street, Baltimore, MD 21230
(301) 659-9314

A membership organization composed of blind people and of interested sighted persons; its purpose is the complete integration of the blind as equals into society. It serves as the voice of the blind and a vehicle for their joint action in all arenas.

Activities: Provides education, information, lobbying, and training for and about blindness and blind people.

Volunteer Opportunities: Welcomes volunteers of any age to help with any of its activities, which vary depending on local current needs, with the only requirement being a willingness to work and to learn about blindness.

Contact: National headquarters for location of nearest chapter.

"The most important thing you can do is to help us spread the new concepts about blindness: we are people, just like you."

NATIONAL MENTAL HEALTH ASSOCIATION
1021 Prince Street, Alexandria, VA 22314
(703) 684–7722

A national organization that works for America's mental health by promoting improved treatment, understanding, and public support of mental illness. One in five Americans yearly suffers from a diagnosable mental disorder, but less than 20 percent receive appropriate treatment and services.

Activities: Through 600 state and local affiliates, staffed primarily by volunteers, advocates the rights of the mentally ill, supports community mental health prevention and treatment services, and works directly to provide aid and training.

Volunteer Opportunities: For anyone of any age with a special interest in mental health or the mentally ill, chapters need help for all activities, from clerical work and events organization to lobbying and visitations.

Contact: National headquarters, or see phone book for local chapter.

> **"Since mental health affects everyone's life and is equally as important as physical fitness in people's overall health, we strive to make mental health a major national priority."**

NATIONAL MULTIPLE SCLEROSIS SOCIETY

205 East 42nd Street, New York, NY 10017
(212) 986–3240

The only nationwide society supporting programs of national and international research in the cause, prevention, cure, and treatment of MS, which is a disabling neurological disease affecting hundreds of thousands of Americans, primarily striking young adults.

Activities: Sponsors research and works to raise public awareness on MS and to aid victims of the disease to cope with its difficulties. Raises funds to support these activities through contests, competitions, dinners, and other events, including a "Readathon."

Volunteer Opportunities: Some 500,000 volunteers nationwide participate in all of the society's activities, primarily through 101 local chapters; Students Against Multiple Sclerosis is active on campuses throughout the country.

Contact: National headquarters for local chapter.

> **"People normally volunteer because they want to pay their civic rent. Volunteers for our organization are concerned about multiple sclerosis, which affects young people and stays with them a lifetime."**

UNITED CEREBRAL PALSY
ASSOCIATIONS, INC.
66 East 34th Street, New York, NY 10016
(212) 481–6347

The only national voluntary agency targeting its services to the specific needs of persons with cerebral palsy, which is a condition caused by damage, usually during birth or early childhood, to the central nervous system.

Activities: Supports research and public education, and provides services that enable disabled people to live independently.

Volunteer Opportunities: Participate in all activities of the organization, including fundraising projects, usually working through state and local affiliates.

Contact: National headquarters for local affiliate.

> **"To fulfill our dual mission of mainstreaming disabled persons and preventing cerebral palsy, volunteers are UCP's most valuable resource."**

OTHER RESOURCES

In addition to the organizations listed here, special-interest groups exist for virtually every disorder—from asthma, allergies, deafness, and mental retardation, to Parkinson's disease. Check the topics in *The Encyclopedia of Associations* for ones that have meaning for *you*.

See also: "Drugs and Alcohol" entries (pages 65–68).

DRUGS AND ALCOHOL

The abuse of alcohol and other drugs is high on the list of direct threats to you and your friends. You probably know someone who has been killed or maimed by some form of addiction or chemical dependency. You have certainly read and heard enough about the dangers to children and teens of drug and alcohol use to be aware of the need for prevention.

It's likely, too, that you have personal knowledge of the *indirect* harm—physical or emotional damage to families, friends, and neighbors—caused by drug and alcohol abuse: Various estimates cite one in four individuals or half the families in this country as affected by some form of addiction.

Overwhelming as the problem can seem, the good news is that, among the "killer diseases," addiction and alcoholism are ones that can be prevented and successfully treated—not with dramatic medical breakthroughs, but with public awareness and community efforts. *You*, as an individual or as part of a group of young people, can be a direct and important part of those efforts. Teenagers in the state of Washington, for example, were able to coordinate segments of their entire community in a mobilization against addiction and its effects. They called themselves "Responsible Educated Adolescents Can Help (REACH)"— and that's what you can do, too, either through groups in which you already are active, or in organizations like the ones listed here.

JUST SAY NO CLUBS
Just Say No Foundation
1777 North California Boulevard
Walnut Creek, CA 94596
(415) 939–6666 or 1–800–285–2766

This antidrug organization originated as a local project by Oakland (CA) Parents in Action, which became a nationwide voluntary, privately funded campaign against drug use.

Activities: Helps to organize "Just Say No" drug-free clubs for young people in schools and communities across the country that work to prevent drug abuse; publicizes, educates, and develops community involvement for drug-free living; organizes fundraising events to support activities.

Volunteer Opportunities: Join a club—or start one—using suggestions mailed from headquarters.

Contact: National headquarters for location of nearest club.

> **"When youth get together, we have youth power. . . . If you can say no to drugs, it's the first step to the beginning of your future."**

TEEN-AGE ASSEMBLY OF AMERICA/ YOUTH AGAINST DRUGS PROJECT
905 Umi Street, Honolulu, HI 96819
(808) 841–1146

Campaign organized by national youth organization to mobilize peer pressure against use of alcohol and drugs.

Activities: Provides information to students in schools throughout the country about signing a pledge against drug use, establishing trained peer-group workshops, and counseling fellow students in staying away from drugs.

Volunteer Opportunities: Join local Youth Against Drugs committee, or form one, using guidelines from headquarters.

Contact: National headquarters.

> **"15% of American youth get drunk weekly; millions use marijuana daily; much drug use begins at earlier ages, and most violent crimes and fatal accidents involving youth are drug-related. Peer pressure is the main reason for youths' drug use—and peer pressure can work *against* drug use."**

OTHER RESOURCES

Although the following groups do not make direct use of young volunteers from outside their organizations, they are excellent sources of information and assistance in the formation of groups related to alcoholism, drug abuse, and other addictions:

ALCOHOL EDUCATION FOR YOUTH AND
COMMUNITY
362 State Street
Albany, NY 12210
(518) 436–9319

ALCOHOLICS ANONYMOUS WORLD SERVICES
P.O. Box 459, Grand Central Station
New York, NY 10163
(212) 686–1100

COCAINE HOTLINE
1–800–COCAINE

NARCOTICS ANONYMOUS
P.O. Box 9999
Van Nuys, CA 91409
(818) 780–3951

NATIONAL ASSOCIATION ON DRUG ABUSE
PROBLEMS
355 Lexington Avenue
New York, NY 10017
(212) 986–1170

NATIONAL COUNCIL ON ALCOHOLISM
12 West 21st Street
New York, NY 10010
(212) 206–6770

See also: Students Against Driving Drunk (page 121).

THE ELDERLY

If you want to feel appreciated, get involved with some senior citizens. A big-city teenager resented being pressured by his church group into paying a call on residents of a neighborhood nursing home. He came away feeling proud, though, because the people he met were so glad to meet *him*—and when he returned the following week, he was pleased to find that the residents had missed him and were looking forward to his visit.

When dealing with older generations of our own families, many of us have the feeling that we can't quite come up to their expectations or demands. We may find it depressing to see what age does to people we remembered as youthful, or we may not enjoy doing what we feel is our duty to older relatives. So we shy away from getting involved with *any* older people.

But reaching out to the elderly who are not related is often a much more rewarding experience—especially when they have no available families of their own. Often, even the smallest service elicits tremendous appreciation.

There are many ways for you, independently or as part of a group, to help the elderly in your community. Teens visit senior-citizen centers or nursing homes to entertain or take gifts, perhaps, to teach crafts and other skills, or just to chat. They carry "Meals on Wheels" to the homebound, or help transport the elderly to doctors' offices. They take turns running errands for an elderly neighbor, or volunteer to do household chores (much more fun for somebody else than for your own family). They serve as escorts for older people, especially at night or in bad weather, or take them to movies and other events (some seniors especially enjoy being a part of school activities). A group or class may "adopt" some senior citizens and help with every aspect of their lives. You can also volunteer to spread the word among older members of the community about the activities of local senior centers, so that all who need them can participate.

If you don't live near an older person or a senior facility, you can check the Yellow Pages under "Senior Citizens," or contact your local government's division on the aging.

However, while you're busy thinking about what you can do for the elderly, don't forget what they can do for *you*. You'll find older people everywhere who are willing, able, and eager to help with *your* projects. They can bring special experience and skills to almost any worthwhile effort you're undertaking as an individual or a group. They have the time available that other adults lack—and many older people especially enjoy helping youth.

The same centers and agencies that can get you involved with helping older people can also direct you to places where you can *recruit* them for your own activities. Or, contact the groups listed here to get an idea of what active seniors can do and where you can find them in your area.

AMERICAN ASSOCIATION OF RETIRED PERSONS (AARP)
1909 K Street, NW, Washington, DC 20049
(202) 872-4700

Nonprofit nonpartisan organization for Americans aged 50 and over, with over 5,000 chapters throughout the country.
Activities: Provides a variety of programs and services to and for its twenty-four million members—from consumer discounts through legislative lobbying. Sponsors "intergenerational activities" toward development of good relations between young and old.
Volunteer Opportunities: Though AARP uses only its own members for volunteer work, young people can use them for their own volunteer projects, and can also join the intergenerational program.
Contact: National headquarters for location of nearest chapter.

> **AARP's motto is "To serve, not to be served."**

RETIRED SENIOR VOLUNTEER
PROGRAM
ACTION
Washington, DC 20525
(202) 634-9353

A government-sponsored organization designed to offer older adults a meaningful life through volunteer service that responds to community needs.

Activities: Mobilizes some 350,000 volunteers in a wide range of local projects, including career counseling for youth, services for latchkey children, crime watches, and tutoring.

Volunteer Opportunities: Though all volunteers are over sixty years of age, young people can help by encouraging older adults to participate in these programs, and can use RSVP volunteers in youth-related programs.

Contact: National headquarters.

> **"Older Americans are a vast, readily available resource and a boon to every community."**

HUNGER AND HOMELESSNESS

The hungry and the homeless used to be only the faraway recipients of our charity. Foreign countries still teem with these desperate people, but in recent years they have been perhaps the most visible signs of need in our own country. In larger cities you can see them, sleeping on the street, or standing in long lines outside of soup kitchens. Elsewhere, you may notice that your school, church, or community center is used as a shelter during the night. This situation is frightening for many, and they may feel threatened by the people they see on the streets around them. Others may feel only despair, because the problem seems too huge to deal with. It is certainly a complex problem, and one that requires the concerted efforts of many private and public agencies to root out.

But in the meantime, what you can do is to help provide food and shelter for the people who lack it in your own community and around the country and the world as well. You can volunteer to work in a local soup kitchen (ask your church, social-services organizations, or local government for locations). You can organize the collection of food, clothing, or funds for donation to a wide variety of agencies for distribution. Or, you can join others in rehabilitating run-down buildings for use as homes.

These efforts will not only provide direct help, but they can snowball. Before the "homeless" became well publicized, for example, a young boy in Philadelphia began going out at night to take food and blankets to the street people; and he inspired imitation among people who had ignored the similar work of older people and more established operations. When adults see you collecting or distributing food, or fixing up old houses, they may well feel compelled to join in and to work in other ways to solve these critical problems.

The organizations listed here are among the many that coordinate aid to the needy in this country and around the world.

CARE

660 First Avenue, New York, NY 10016
(212) 686–3110

The world's largest nonsectarian, nongovernmental, nonprofit development and relief organization, whose purpose is to help the world's poor help themselves to achieve social and economic well-being.

Activities: Distributes food, services, health supplies, and equipment to needy communities in thirty-seven countries; trains and coordinates local participants in improvement projects; responds to disasters with relief supplies and workers.

Volunteer Opportunities: Help with clerical and other tasks in national and regional offices; participate in special events that publicize and raise funds; on your own or with a group, raise funds, collect food for international work and disaster relief.

Contact: Headquarters for location of nearest chapter.

> **"Anyone concerned can help to end hunger and save the lives of children and entire communities around the world."**

FOOD FOR THE HUNGRY, INC.
P.O. Box E, Scottsdale, AZ 85260
1–800–2–HUNGER

A nonprofit Christian charitable organization that offers disaster relief and long-range self-help assistance to people in need throughout the world.

Activities: Sends food and initiates development programs through international Hunger Corps of trained volunteers.

Volunteer Opportunities: Hunger Corps volunteers must be at least 21 years old; however, 150,000 volunteers are used to collect food and funds and to publicize efforts, individually and through churches nationwide.

Contact: National headquarters.

> **"The effect of hunger on people is enormous. Yet, they die one at a time, so we can help them one at a time."**

HABITAT FOR HUMANITY
Habitat and Church Streets
Americus, GA 31709
(912) 924-6935

A nonprofit Christian housing ministry that works in partnership with people in need to improve the conditions in which they are forced to live.

Activities: Works, directly and through affiliates, with needy people in projects around the world, including the United States, to build and rebuild homes and communities.

Volunteer Opportunities: Almost all work is done by volunteers, both on construction projects and in administrative offices at international headquarters in Georgia. Volunteers must be at least eighteen for U.S. service (twenty-one for overseas) and in most cases be able to commit at least three months to a project, although requirements of local affiliates may vary.

Contact: International headquarters.

> **"The ministry of Habitat binds people together by the common goal of working to provide decent housing for and with God's people in need."**

SECOND HARVEST
343 South Dearborn, Chicago, IL 60604
(312) 341–1303

A national network of privately funded food banks—surplus foods and grocery products gathered from manufacturers and stores—for distribution to organizations that feed the nation's hungry.

Activities: Solicits donations from national companies, distributes it to over 200 certified food banks throughout the country, and through them to 30,000 charitable feeding programs.

Volunteer Opportunities: Work at food bank nearest you, performing clerical, warehouse, and other work.

Contact: National headquarters for location of nearest food bank.

> **"In the land of plenty, plenty of us are hungry—Second Harvest offers solutions."**

OTHER RESOURCES

While the following organization does not use volunteers directly, it serves as a clearinghouse for information on the homeless, and could direct interested volunteers to agencies where they could help.

NATIONAL COALITION FOR THE HOMELESS
105 East 22nd Street
New York, NY 10010
(212) 460–8110

1620 I Street, NW
Washington, DC 20006
(202) 659–3310

311 South Spring Street
Los Angeles, CA 90013
(213) 488–9137

See also: "Social-Service Organizations" entries (pages 123–129) for groups that provide food, shelter, and other assistance.

ILLITERACY

You can read—you're reading this. Imagine what your life would be like if you couldn't. Try buying food without knowing what the labels say, or finding your way around a new part of town without being able to read the street signs. And you can't find a job if you can't read the want ads or fill out the applications. *Millions* of Americans live that way—and around the world, the most modern technology is worthless against disease and starvation without people to read the instructions.

Because you can read, you can teach others to do it. Though illiterate adults are more comfortable learning from adults, there are many people your own age and younger who can use your help. Recent immigrants or refugees may be literate, but only in their own languages—you can help them to read English. Younger students in your school system will learn better with the kind of individual help you can offer.

Your school or public library may have a learn-to-read program that will provide you with the support you need to be a reading teacher. Check it out, and if neither has a literacy project, you can help to start one with the aid of the organizations listed here. Whether you want to teach reading or not, you can get involved in the fight against illiteracy by working to support and publicize these groups.

LAUBACH LITERACY
INTERNATIONAL
1320 Jamesville Avenue, Syracuse, NY 13210
(315) 422-9121

The nation's largest network of adult literacy programs providing reading instruction in 600 communities throughout the country. Some 26 million Americans are functionally illiterate, with their numbers increased each year by about 1 million school dropouts; Laubach volunteers teach about 60,000 adults a year. It is also an excellent source of information about illiteracy.

Activities: Trains tutors for individual and small-group teaching of adults with low or no English-language reading skills; trains and coordinates leaders for local groups; educates the public about literacy programs; publishes materials for new adult readers.

Volunteer Opportunities: Primarily uses adults as tutors, although some Laubach material may be used in peer-group projects. Older teens or college-age students serve as tutors. All tutors are trained. Volunteers of all ages can help with distributing information and providing backup services.

Contact: National headquarters, or see phone book for local chapter.

> **"The problem of illiteracy is receiving national attention. Volunteers in our programs can have an impact on that problem in a very personal way—and they can truly make a difference in another person's life."**

LITERACY VOLUNTEERS
OF AMERICA, INC.

5795 Widewaters Parkway, Syracuse, NY 13214
(315) 445-8000

A national organization that works to combat the problem of adult illiteracy through the enlistment and training of a huge pool of volunteer tutors.

Activities: With over 200 affiliates throughout the country, develops materials and trains volunteers to teach illiterate or non-English speaking adults to read.

Volunteer Opportunities: Tutors should be over eighteen, but some local groups may use younger students in peer tutoring, and volunteers of all ages can support program in other ways, as well as use organization as a resource.

Contact: National headquarters, or see phone book for local chapter.

"Learning to read gives illiterate adults a new sense of self-worth—and our volunteers say that they get as much as they give."

READING IS FUNDAMENTAL, INC. (RIF)

600 Maryland Avenue, SW
Smithsonian Institution
Washington, DC 20560
(202) 287–3220

A national nonprofit organization that has worked with local groups since 1966 to promote reading among American young people.

Activities: Community groups formed according to RIF guidelines select and buy books for children who otherwise might not have books to choose and own. Also develop book-related activities to reinforce children's desire to read.

Volunteer Opportunities: Work with local groups to raise funds and to plan and participate in activities related to children's books and reading.

Contact: National headquarters for local affiliate.

> **"Children who can choose and keep books discover for themselves that reading is both enjoyable and important."**

INTERNATIONAL COOPERATION

Many people get to see the world; others have the chance to see *and understand* it. That's what you can do—and experience a fantastic adventure, too—when you get involved with groups that sponsor international exchanges of young people. This is travel with a purpose: Volunteers help to perform useful services in the countries they visit. And beyond that immediate purpose is the understanding that comes from living and working with people of other cultures—an understanding that can help to foster the kind of harmony that can insure a future for the world.

Besides that, it *is* an adventure. And is it fun? As one teen reported after a summer in an overseas workcamp, "My friends asked me, 'Did you have fun?' I didn't know what to say. Fun wasn't the point. It wasn't fun—it was the best experience of my life." Sure, it's fun.

But if you personally don't like the idea, there are many ways you can work toward international understanding without leaving home. You can welcome foreign students into your home or community, and you can support the organizations that share these goals. The ones in this section can show you how.

COUNCIL ON INTERNATIONAL
EDUCATIONAL EXCHANGE

205 East 42nd Street, New York, NY 10017
(212) 661-1414

Volunteer Projects:
356 West 34th Street, New York, NY 10001
(212) 695-0291

A private nonprofit membership organization concerned with international education and student travel.

Activities: Provides a wide variety of services for student travel, from information and publications to budget tours, including scholarships and a placement service for international volunteer projects both abroad and in the United States.

Volunteer Opportunities: Placement (for a low fee) in a two- to four-week international community-service work project in Europe, Canada, or at a multinational site in the United States, during the summer months. Room and board provided; participants supply transportation, but some scholarships are available. Minimum age is eighteen, except for projects in West Germany, which accept sixteen-year-olds.

Contact: National headquarters.

> **"If you are flexible, outgoing, ready for a challenge and have a sense of humor, a volunteer project may be the ideal way for you to travel."**

THE EXPERIMENT
IN INTERNATIONAL LIVING
Kipling Road, Brattleboro, VT 05301
1-800-451-4456

A private nonprofit organization that for over fifty years has been sponsoring visits by students (and others) to the United States and abroad.

Activities: Coordinates and sponsors summer- or semester-long homestay visits to twenty-three countries for American high school and college students, and U.S. homestays for visitors from abroad.

Volunteer Opportunities: Visit a foreign family (for a fee), or encourage your family or other families in your community to be hosts for exchange visits by individuals, families, and especially other high school students.

Contact: National headquarters.

> **"The homestay experience can be a great
> adventure for you and your family."**

GROUND ZERO PAIRING PROJECT
P.O. Box 19329, Portland, OR 97219
(503) 245–3519

Nonpartisan nonadvocacy educational organization that works to involve the American people in efforts to prevent the threat of nuclear war.

Activities: Produces and distributes games, books, and educational material for use in schools and communities; promotes establishment of community and school connections with communities in the Soviet Union.

Volunteer Opportunities: Join or organize an effort in school to send a "community portrait" to a similar town or city in the Soviet Union.

Contact: National headquarters.

"Make the first strike a knock on the door."

INTERNATIONAL CHRISTIAN YOUTH EXCHANGE

U.S. Committee: 134 West 26th Street
New York, NY 10001
(212) 206–7307

An international organization whose purpose is the exchange of young people of any faith among its twenty-six participating countries.

Activities: Sponsors and coordinates homestay and study visits abroad for American students and others, and for foreign visitors to the United States; arranges and supervises international voluntary service programs.

Volunteer Opportunities: Participate in voluntary social-service projects abroad (minimum age from sixteen to twenty, depending on the country); encourage your family or others in your community to host visitors from abroad. Participants may be of any (or no) religious faith, but should feel committed to the organization's goals of international understanding.

Contact: National headquarters.

> **"ICYE is committed to breaking through barriers between cultures and peoples and working for justice for all persons."**

Mid-Valley School District Senior High School Library

OPEN DOOR STUDENT EXCHANGE
124 East Merrick Road
Valley Stream, NY 11582
(516) 825–8485

A nonprofit international educational-exchange organization providing intercultural learning opportunities for high school students and their families.

Activities: For a fee that includes international transportation arranges short- and long-term educational programs for U.S. high school students in countries around the world; arranges homestay visits in the United States for students from abroad. Scholarships are available.

Volunteer Opportunities: Apply for foreign visits, or encourage your family to host a visiting high school student.

Contact: National headquarters.

> **"Open Door volunteer opportunities provide a deeply personal vehicle for enjoying and learning about other cultures."**

OPERATION CROSSROADS AFRICA, INC.

150 Fifth Avenue, New York, NY 10011
(212) 242–8550
1–800–422–3742 (outside of New York state)

A nonprofit organization that for over thirty years has sent volunteers to work in community-service programs in Africa and the Caribbean.

Activities: Sponsors and arranges volunteer work camp projects in thirty-five African and twenty Caribbean countries; brings leaders and professionals from Africa and the Caribbean to consult in the United States; sponsors medical and agricultural projects abroad.

Volunteer Opportunities: For a fee (which can be raised by community contributions), high school students may participate in the Caribbean Work Camp Program; raise funds and collect goods for the organization's service work.

Contact: National headquarters.

> **"The most important task in a shrinking world is the bringing of people into contact with people across all the old crumbling barriers of nation, culture, and race."**

SERVICE CIVIL INTERNATIONAL USA (SCI-USA)

Innisfree Village, Crozet, VA 22932

A nonprofit voluntary organization dedicated to the promotion of peace through international work camps. SCI-USA is the American branch of an international organization that was founded in 1920 and serves as a consultant to UNESCO and the Council of Europe.

Activities: Sponsors work camps in over thirty countries, where groups of people from diverse backgrounds perform both manual work (such as construction, renovation, or forestry) and social service (such as leading children's day camps or programs for the elderly).

Volunteer Opportunities: Anyone over sixteen may volunteer for short-term summer work camps in the United States; anyone over eighteen may participate in short- and long-term work camps throughout Europe and the United States. No special skills needed. A small application fee is required, and volunteers pay travel expenses.

Contact: National headquarters.

> **"SCI provides a way for people of different countries to develop close friendships in the process of doing valuable community service."**

VOLUNTEERS FOR PEACE
INTERNATIONAL WORKCAMPS
Tiffany Road, Belmont, VT 05730
(802) 259-2759

Volunteers for Peace is a nonprofit membership corporation that coordinates international work camps in the United States and abroad as a way to work toward practical and humane ways to prevent and resolve world conflict.

Activities: Arranges and provides placement for work camps in thirty-six countries, with cooperation from agencies here and abroad.

Volunteer Opportunities: For a low registration fee, participate in community-service work camps abroad or in the United States (minimum age eighteen for most areas, fourteen to sixteen for some; volunteers provide transportation); help organize a community group to host a work camp here.

Contact: National headquarters.

> **"This is your chance to promote global harmony in a personal and meaningful way by demonstrating your commitment to other human beings."**

VOLUNTEERS IN MISSION
475 Riverside Drive, Room 1126
New York, NY 10115
(212) 870-2767

A service of the Program Agency of the United Presbyterian Church, to provide educational, medical, and other forms of help in the United States and abroad.

Activities: At the request of local churches or church-related institutions, sponsors and coordinates volunteer projects for people of all ages for periods of a few weeks to two years.

Volunteer Opportunities: High school students are eligible to participate in one- and two-week work camps; Presbyterian membership not required, but participants are expected to share Christian ideals.

Contact: National headquarters.

"Through Christian service, many people have profound experiences of growth—in faith and in awareness."

OTHER RESOURCES

The groups listed in this section are some of the ones that sponsor free or *fairly* low-cost projects; your religious or social group may also. Because others require what seems a hefty outlay of funds from their participants—though they're quite legitimate—you'll want to check out any international program carefully.

For information, contact:

THE AMERICAN YOUTH WORK CENTER
1522 Connecticut Avenue, NW
Washington, DC 20036
(202) 328–3052

This organization works regularly with international exchange programs.

INTERNATIONAL EDUCATION INFORMATION CENTER
809 United Nations Plaza
New York, NY 10017
(212) 984–5413

It provides information based on the resources of the Institute of International Education, the largest agency of its kind in the country.

And check the reference books listed on page 149.

NATURE AND THE ENVIRONMENT

This summer, hundreds of teens are planning to live and work in the wilderness because they love nature and the outdoor life. Hundreds of others who will have the same kind of summer have never even been camping before, but they will also help achieve the goal of protecting and maintaining our natural resources—while enjoying the kind of group experience they could never get at home. Some of the groups listed here offer that kind of opportunity.

Maybe, though, you're like many others who realize the importance of a clean and secure environment but have no interest at all in roughing it. You, too, can make a contribution without setting foot in the woods, as you'll learn from the entries here.

Nature exists on a small scale, as well. On your own or with your neighbors or service group, you can plant trees on your block or start a community garden. If you're also concerned with young, old, or handicapped people, you can get them involved in a garden, or organize them into a mini nature corps, working to protect the environment where *you* live.

AMERICAN FORESTRY ASSOCIATION
1319 18th Street, NW
Washington, DC 20036
(202) 467–5810 or 1–800–368–5748

A national nongovernmental citizens' conservation organization with 45,000 professional and lay members, dedicated to the protection and wise management of trees and forests through encouraging local participation in environmental decisions before there is a need for lawsuits or legislation.

Activities: Promotes public awareness of the role of forests and other natural resources through publications, field trips, and awards; encourages individuals and communities to become active in dealing with environmental issues.

Volunteer Opportunities: Join or help to form a "Friends of Trees" group to focus on local problems of conservation and ecological protection.

Contact: National headquarters.

> **"Today's world fairly bubbles with controversial resource issues. Trees are crucial to the earth's ecology, and we believe that it takes an educated, sensitive, and involved citizenry to strike the right balance between preservation and use of trees and forests."**

Mid-Valley School District
Senior High School Library

DEFENDERS OF WILDLIFE
1244 19th Street, NW
Washington, DC 20036
(202) 659–9510

A national nonprofit organization formed in 1947 to reform cruel trapping practices, and now working to preserve, enhance, and protect wildlife—individual endangered species as well as total natural ecosystems.

Activities: Supports research and uses education, publications, lobbying, litigation, and activist involvement toward the protection of endangered wildlife, endangered habitats and non-game wildlife, and the prevention of wildlife damage.

Volunteer Opportunities: Anyone over the age of fifteen can help with clerical, research, and public-contact work in national or regional offices. Or become a member and join in letter-writing campaigns or work with network of "grass-roots activists" in more intensive lobbying activities.

Contact: National headquarters for location of nearest chapter.

> **"Volunteers not only help improve wildlife protection, but also learn about wildlife, meet new people, learn how a conservation organization works, and have fun."**

ENVIRONMENTAL DEFENSE FUND
257 Park Avenue South, New York, NY 10010
(212) 505–2100

A national nonpartisan public-interest group with 50,000 professional and lay members dedicated to developing and promoting creative solutions to environmental problems through a partnership of science and law.

Activities: Working through national and regional offices, supports research and promotes legislation to purify water sources, stop acid rain, protect wildlife, and remove toxic chemicals from the environment. Maintains a computerized national information-exchange network.

Volunteer Opportunities: Actively seeking volunteers to organize and participate in fundraising events and lobbying efforts. Also, hires high school and college students to work either for hourly pay or school credit as aides in national or regional offices.

Contact: National headquarters or these regional offices:

1616 P Street, NW
Washington, DC 20036
(202) 387–3500

2606 Dwight Way
Berkeley, CA 94704
(415) 548–8906

1405 Arapahoe Avenue
Boulder, CO 80302
(303) 440–4901

1108 East Main Street
Richmond, VA 23219
(804) 780–1297

> **"Working here, with the dedication and expertise of the staff, is inspiring and educational. One gets the feeling that we *are* making a difference—that there are things that each one of us can do to reverse the course of environmental degradation."**

FOREST SERVICE
U.S. Department of Agriculture
Box 96090, Washington, DC 20013
(202) 535-0927

A branch of the Department of Agriculture that is devoted to the management, protection, and use of the nation's forests and rangelands, which comprise almost two-thirds of America's territory.

Activities: Supports research in forestry, and works with public and private foresters and agencies to focus on the scientific management of forest systems and their water, wildlife, and minerals, and to educate the public in the use, protection, and enjoyment of forests.

Volunteer Opportunities: An active and well-organized volunteer program throughout the country for all ages (parental consent required for those under eighteen). Wide scope of activities, both indoor and outdoor, including clerical, research, and public-contact work, as well as maintenance, construction, conservation, and tour-guide services. Makes a formal record of volunteer's activities, provides a Certificate of Appreciation, and grants college credits in some cases.

Contact: National headquarters, or see phone book under "U.S. Government, Dept. of Agriculture, Forest Service" for location of nearest field office.

> **"Offers anyone who wants to become involved the opportunity to promote conservation and wise use of America's land."**

GREENPEACE USA
1611 Connecticut Avenue, NW
Washington, DC 20009
(202) 462–1177

American arm of an international network of ecologists and the ecologically concerned, working to promote international activities and agreements on protection of the global ecosystem, including reduction of environmental poisoning, unnecessary slaughter of wildlife, and reliance on nuclear weapons.

Activities: Works toward awareness raising and the accomplishment of environmental safety goals through nonviolent direct action, lobbying, fundraising, research, and public information.

Volunteer Opportunities: Join "activist networks" in phone, letter, education, and petition campaigns on toxics, wildlife, and/or disarmament projects.

Contact: National headquarters for location of nearest chapter.

> **"All forms of life are interconnected and interdependent, and we have learned that we must respect the diversity of life as we respect ourselves."**

INTERNATIONAL TREE PROJECT
DC2—Room 1103, United Nations
New York, NY 10017
(212) 754-3123

A combined international effort coordinated through the United Nations to combat the problem of global deforestation.

Activities: Encourages the planting and care of trees in communities and regions throughout the world; educates the public on the need for protecting natural resources.

Volunteer Opportunities: Plant a tree and care for it, and encourage others to do the same.

Contact: National headquarters.

> **"A tree you plant and nurture can enhance the natural environment while providing useful products."**

NATIONAL AUDUBON SOCIETY
950 Third Avenue, New York, NY 10022
(212) 832–3200

National organization with over half a million volunteers/members dedicated to the long-term protection and wise use of natural resources, and to the solution of problems created by their depletion.

Activities: Supports environmental research; maintains wildlife sanctuaries; promotes ecological education; works for beneficial legislation on environmental issues.

Volunteer Opportunities: Work through local and regional offices on their ongoing environmental projects, including workshops, camps, lobbying, and education. Internship program, by application: for students, preferably college students but at least of legal working age, in Washington, DC, office and in wildlife sanctuaries in Maine, Kentucky, Florida, South Carolina, and Connecticut; living expenses paid; college credit offered.

Contact: National headquarters, or see phone book for local chapter.

> **"Volunteers are the heart and soul of our work to maintain and improve the quality of life on earth for ourselves and future generations."**

NATIONAL PARK SERVICE
19th & C Streets, NW, Washington, DC 20240
(202) 343-7394

An agency of the U.S. federal government administering over 300 national parks, seashores, recreation areas, monuments, battlefields, and historic sites in both rural and urban areas of every state, mandated both to conserve and to provide public enjoyment of these sites.

Activities: Protects and maintains all aspects of federal parklands and sites; educates and supervises visitors to them.

Volunteer Opportunities: Diverse, depending on interests and capabilities of volunteer and needs at site—from maintenance of wilderness trails and recreation facilities to guiding tours at historic sites. Thoroughly organized through Volunteers in Parks (VIP) system, which provides training, supervision, and benefits of volunteers. Service is documented; volunteers receive Certificate of Appreciation. Parental consent required for those under eighteen.

Contact: National headquarters, or Division of Visitor Services at regional offices; or VIP coordinator at local sites (see phone book under "US Government—National Park Service").

> **"Many parks owe their very existence to volunteers, and today volunteers are involved in every aspect of their operation through activities that provide a needed public service as well as practical benefits to the volunteer."**

THE NATURE CONSERVANCY
1800 North Kent Street, Arlington, VA 22209
(703) 841–5300

A national nonprofit scientific and educational organization dedicated to preserving the natural diversity in the United States and Latin America.

Activities: Works with paid professionals and volunteers to identify natural areas that best represent the finest components of the natural world; to protect directly and encourage the protection of habitats and ecosystems; and to manage nearly 1,000 preserves owned by the Conservancy.

Volunteer Opportunities: Work through regional divisions, state chapters, and field offices on anything from fundraising and administrative support to maintenance of Conservancy preserves.

Contact: National headquarters for location of field offices.

> **"There is no doubt at all about the need for conservation of our fast diminishing natural lands and the rare and endangered species they shelter."**

NEW ALCHEMY INSTITUTE
237 Hatchville Road, East Falmouth, MA 02536
(617) 563–2655

A small nonprofit research and education center dedicated to promoting the wise stewardship of the earth's resources through sustainable technologies in food production and energy conservation.

Activities: Researches, demonstrates, and teaches organic gardening, aquaculture, solar greenhouse design, solar and super-insulated building design, and ecologically sound pest management on a twelve-acre farm site; supports similar projects throughout the United States and abroad.

Volunteer Opportunities: Participate in all activities at farm; help with promotional and educational activities; serve as an intern or apprentice (by application) for periods from one month to one year; or seek information on starting similar projects locally.

Contact: National headquarters.

> **"We believe that humanity can and must live in a more gentle, environmentally sound manner. Volunteers play an important role in helping us to devise new and productive ways to provide food, energy, and shelter."**

SIERRA CLUB
730 Polk Street, San Francisco, CA 94109
(415) 776–2211

A national organization of over 350,000 members/volunteers joined in efforts to explore, enjoy, and preserve the nation's forests, waters, wildlife, and wilderness.

Activities: Supports research; educates public; lobbies and campaigns for legislation and other actions to save and protect natural resources; involves communities in outings and projects that focus on the environment.

Volunteer Opportunities: With membership, join in "grass-roots" activism of chapters and groups to work on local conservation projects.

Contact: National headquarters, or see phone book for local chapter.

> **"The issues facing us are quite serious: acid rain, clean air and water, safe disposal of toxic wastes, safe sources of energy. The Sierra Club is committed to doing something here and now—and we have a successful record of getting things done."**

STUDENT CONSERVATION ASSOCIATION, INC.

P.O. Box 550, Charlestown, NH 03603
(603) 826–5206

A national nonprofit organization formed in 1947 to bring the energies and abilities of high school and college youth to the aid of public and private agencies responsible for natural resource, conservation, and recreation lands.

Activities: Works with the U.S. National Park Service, Bureau of Land Management, Fish & Wildlife Service, and Forest Service, as well as state agencies and nonprofit organizations, to place students in useful outdoor work projects. In 1987, placed nearly 1,100 volunteers—international students, native Americans, urban disadvantaged youth, and some in special programs for the hearing-impaired.

Volunteer Opportunities: Admission to the program, for those sixteen and older, is competitive and by application; acceptance is based on equal-opportunity guidelines, but groups are chosen to represent a variety of geographic and economic backgrounds. Groups, led by experienced supervisors, live and work for three to four weeks in wilderness areas, participating in such projects as trail maintenance, bridge building, and restoration. No previous experience in camping is required for high school work groups; food and shelter is provided, and financial aid is available for those who cannot pay travel costs to the site.

Contact: National headquarters.

> **"Volunteers receive an outdoor education and group-living and work experience which provides them with skills that help them to qualify for jobs, and enables them to be better informed and active citizens, while caring for our nation's lands."**

OTHER RESOURCES

These organizations can give you ideas for environmental projects—ones that you can start on your own, or ones in your area that you can join:

CENTER FOR ENVIRONMENTAL EDUCATION
624 9th Street, NW
Washington, DC 20001
(202) 737–3600

CHILDREN OF THE GREEN EARTH
Box 95219
Seattle, WA 98145
(206) 525–4002

Or ask your local 4-H club or U.S. Department of Agriculture Extension Service for ideas. Their telephone numbers are in the phone book.

POLITICS AND GOVERNMENT

Sally is thirteen and a political activist. She couldn't vote, of course, but she could volunteer to work for a congressional campaign. She did, and they were glad to have her. Now, she's got the political "bug," and with the experience she already has, she's an effective worker for community campaigns that use the political system to attain their goals.

In this section are the two major national political parties, which may welcome your help at some level and that can offer unbeatable opportunities for learning about the political process from the inside. There are many other political parties, of course: If you want to volunteer in politics, you'll want to find the party that most closely matches your own ideas.

But party politics isn't the only game in town. Almost all of the groups listed in this book deal with politics in some way, since they often must rely on government or other major organizations for at least part of their support. If you're interested in politics, you can help them with their lobbying activities; or, like Sally, you can become active in local and community betterment campaigns, which require the same kind of politicking that goes on in Washington.

Through other kinds of groups, you can learn about—and have an impact on—the workings of government. One of those is listed here, and many youth organizations include projects to meet with their mayors, and state and national representatives. If yours doesn't, why not suggest it? It's a way of making your voice heard that most adults can't equal.

Your activism can be strictly nonpartisan: Many service groups assist in voter-registration campaigns, for example—important contributions to a healthy society.

Like it or not (and you may *love* it), politics is what makes our system work, so the more you can do about it—the more you can learn about it—the better off we all are. Why wait to vote when you can get involved now?

CLOSE UP FOUNDATION
1235 Jefferson Davis Highway
Arlington, VA 22202
1-800-336-5479 or (703) 892-5400

The largest government-studies program in the country; a non-partisan nonprofit group dedicated to the principle that active, aware citizens are essential to a responsive government and a healthy community.

Activities: Brings students, teachers, and older Americans to Washington, DC, for face-to-face meetings with government leaders, and to Williamsburg, VA, for study of early institutions; promotes relevant civics education through school programs and materials; sponsors regional, state, and local programs for discussion of current issues.

Volunteer Opportunities: In over 3,000 high schools throughout the country, students help volunteer Close-Up teachers to organize fundraising, educational, and travel activities; tenth-, eleventh-, and twelfth-grade students can join with others in community Close-Up groups for travel and seminar programs.

Contact: National headquarters.

> **"I will never forget what I learned on Close Up: that what I say and do as a citizen does make a difference."**

YOUNG DEMOCRATS OF AMERICA
Democratic National Committee
430 South Capitol Street, SE
Washington, DC 20003
(202) 863–8000

National organization with regional and state chapters for the encouragement of young people's involvement in government affairs and the political process, and to promote the principles of the Democratic party.

Activities: Through local clubs, participates in voter-registration drives, voter education and publicity, campaigns for local, state, and national candidates; organizes interest-group coalitions and fundraising activities.

Volunteer Opportunities: Join or form a community or campus club; membership is open to any Democrat between sixteen and thirty-five years of age.

Contact: National headquarters for location of nearest chapter.

> **"Join us in making young people heard on all levels of government and political activity."**

YOUNG REPUBLICAN NATIONAL FEDERATION

440 First Street, NW, Washington, DC 20003
(202) 662–1340

An auxiliary of the Republican National Committee, working to promote the principles and ideas of the Republican party.
Activities: Supports campaigns for Republican candidates and issues on the local, state, and national level.
Volunteer Opportunities: Members must be over eighteen; work in all activities through local, state, and regional groups.
Contact: National headquarters for location of nearest chapter.

> **"Much of our party's past success can be attributed to the diligent and dedicated efforts of Young Republicans around the country."**

OTHER RESOURCES

A number of organizations exist to promote *non*partisan political activities, like voter registration and information, or campaign debates. Among the best established of these is:

LEAGUE OF WOMEN VOTERS OF THE U.S.
1730 M Street, NW
Washington, DC 20036
(202) 429–1965
or see phone book for local chapter

(It is not for women only.)

PRISONERS

Societies imprison people to get them away from society. That may seem obvious, but think about this: The very isolation from society contributes to the problems that prisoners have and cause when they return to society. The families that prisoners, no matter what their crimes, leave behind often become innocent victims who also create problems in society.

Some very simple steps can help ease these human and social difficulties. Try to imagine being locked up in a cell for whatever reason, then think what a communication from the outside world would mean, or how reassuring it would be to know that your mother or little brother was getting some of the support and companionship you couldn't offer. Through groups like the ones listed here, you can make this simple difference for a prisoner.

Sometimes, in this country and others, people are imprisoned unfairly. If that bothers you, you can also take a small action that can make a big difference—and in the process, you'll gain a deeper understanding of what "justice" means to *you*.

AMNESTY INTERNATIONAL USA
322 Eighth Avenue, New York, NY 10001
(212) 807–8400

The American arm of an international nonpartisan organization that works specifically for the release of "prisoners of conscience" (nonviolent political prisoners) throughout the world, for their fair and prompt trials, and for the elimination of torture and execution of all prisoners. There are over 500,000 members in 150 countries.

Activities: Writes letters, publicizes, and organizes actions on behalf of individual prisoners of conscience; maintains and circulates files on such cases; organizes campaigns for special situations.

Volunteer Opportunities: Join or form a group in your community or school; as an individual or group, "adopt" a specific prisoner; write letters or telegrams as an individual.

Contact: National headquarters for location of nearest chapter.

> **"Our primary tools—the letter and telegram—are remarkable for their power and simplicity. Sometimes a single letter is enough to improve a prisoner's situation."**

FRIENDS OUTSIDE

116 East San Luis Street, Salinas, CA 93901
(408) 758–2733

Nonprofit organization with nineteen chapters in California, Nevada, and Idaho, dedicated to providing a variety of services for prisoners and their families.

Activities: Services provided include emergency food and clothing, child care, transportation, prison visits, and activities for prisoners' children.

Volunteer Opportunities: Vary from chapter to chapter, as do requirements for volunteers; young volunteers' activities likely to be limited.

Contact: National headquarters.

"Family ties can prevent repeated crime by released prisoners, yet families of prisoners are unfairly victimized and often in great need. Prisoners' children are criminally prone, but Friends Outside can break the cycle of crime."

OTHER RESOURCES

For ideas and information on other ways to aid prisoners, contact:

NATIONAL ASSOCIATION ON VOLUNTEERS IN
CRIMINAL JUSTICE
Wilmington College
Wilmington, OH 45177
(513) 382–6661

This is a coordinating organization committed to the improvement of the juvenile- and criminal-justice systems through citizen participation.

TEENAGERS

Often, the best help for teenagers with problems comes from other teens, and both the helped and the helper stand to gain great reward from this kind of peer interaction. Teens trust other teens to deal straight with them about drugs, family problems, health crises, school failure, or trouble with the law—so you won't need to look far to find ways to help your fellows.

You can **tutor**. You can help another student get by in any subjects where you feel competent—and it will help *your* studies, too. Check for tutoring programs in your own school or in other schools in your area. If there aren't any, try to interest a group in your school or community in organizing one.

How about a **hotline**? At the end of a phone line, you can help other teens with their troubles by listening and by referring them to professional help where necessary. Be sure that any organization with which you sign on offers enough training and backup to make you feel comfortable and competent.

Be a friendly **visitor**. Some kids are so disabled that they can't leave home, or have long-term illnesses that keep them in the hospital. They need all the outside contact they can get with people of their own age, and sometimes, sadly, their old friends forget them. If you have regular time to spend one-on-one this way, ask around or call the adolescent unit of your local hospital.

Seek out **support groups**. If you've been through some major trouble in your life—a family, health, or personal crisis—you can help others who are facing the same things, just by sharing your experiences. If you don't already know of any, check your local hospitals, religious centers, or social-service agencies.

In many communities, **teen centers** exist that are more than hangouts or social groups. They provide counseling, shelter, tutoring, training, even medical and legal help for young people in trouble or with troubles. This is the kind of place where you could both give and gain a lot.

If you want to give your time to teens less fortunate than yourself but you don't know where to turn, check the Yellow

Pages under "Youth" for groups whose activities interest you.

Here are some national organizations that work with teen problems. Even those without local offices can give you help and ideas for your own project.

NATIONAL RUNAWAY SWITCHBOARD

2210 North Halsted Street, Chicago, IL 60614
(312) 880–9860
Youth Service Line: 1–800–621–4000

Operated from Chicago by Metro-Help, Inc., a youth-service agency offering twenty-four-hour, toll-free telephone programs to help teens and children throughout the country solve a variety of problems.

Activities: Responds to 150,000 calls a year from teens (and those concerned about them) who are runaways, are thinking about running away from home, suffer from abuse or drug problems, or are considering suicide. Provides direct, confidential help and support, and maintains a national network of local services to which it refers callers.

Volunteer Opportunities: Uses over 200 volunteers of all ages at its Chicago-based phone lines. Volunteers must attend forty hours of training during a four-week period and commit a minimum of either six hours a week for four months or four hours a week for six months. A good resource for information on groups that provide similar services from other areas.

Contact: National headquarters.

> **"Metro-Help volunteers care—and they do something about it."**

RUNAWAY HOTLINE
P.O. Box 12428, Austin, TX 78711
(512) 463–1980
Hotlines: 1–800–392–3352 in Texas
1–800–231–6946 elsewhere

A toll-free national telephone service for runaway children and teens, operated from state offices in Austin, Texas.

Activities: Acts as a neutral, confidential intermediary to relay messages between runaway children and their families; provides runaways with confidential referrals to needed services.

Volunteer Opportunities: After training, volunteers answer phones in Austin; help is needed throughout the country to publicize the service and raise funds to support it.

Contact: National headquarters.

> **"The Runaway Hotline makes a tremendous difference in the lives of runaway children and their families—but it needs your support and participation."**

STUDENTS AGAINST DRIVING DRUNK (SADD)

P.O. Box 800, Marlboro, MA 01752
(617) 481–3568

A national organization whose purpose is to organize students to combat one of the major killers of their age group: death due to drinking and driving. It works to eliminate drunk driving; to alert students and the community to the dangers of driving under the influence of alcohol and other drugs; and to organize peer counseling for students concerned about alcohol and drug problems.

Activities: Initiates school programs on drinking and driving; organizes SADD chapters in junior highs, high schools, and colleges; distributes and promotes "contracts for life" designed to prevent drunken driving; generates community awareness and support for sober driving.

Volunteer opportunities: Join one of 10,000 local chapters; help to form a chapter; sign and distribute "contracts for life."

Contact: National headquarters for location of nearest chapter.

> **"SADD is a proven lifesaving program because it is student motivated. No one believes that drinking and driving is a good combination. Through SADD, students can now take a leadership role in preventing alcohol-related deaths and injuries."**

OTHER RESOURCES

To find or form other projects that help adolescents, contact:

AMERICAN YOUTH WORK CENTER
1522 Connecticut Avenue, NW
Washington, DC 20036
(202) 328–3052

The Center serves as a clearinghouse for expertise on forming and maintaining programs that deal with a variety of youth-related problems and activities, including health, runaways, crime, addiction, employment, and international exchange. Produces and distributes informational publications.

You might also want to join with people your age in social-service organizations (see pages 123–129) or religious youth groups, or in national organizations like the Scouts.

See also: "Drugs and Alcohol" (pages 65–68) and "International Cooperation" (pages 83–93) entries.

SOCIAL-SERVICE ORGANIZATIONS

By now, you may have become convinced that you want to get involved, but (1) you simply can't think of what you'd like to do; (2) you still feel overwhelmed by the needs you see; or (3) you prefer to support social causes at a bit of a distance. In any case, the groups in this section are the place to turn.

These are organizations that provide a variety of social services in this country and around the world. While you may not be able to volunteer directly for some of them, you can help to support them, either on your own or through groups to which you belong. They may be groups whose help you can enlist in solving a social problem that concerns you in your own community. And they give you an idea of the kinds of things that people are doing to help other people. Not only can you help people through these groups, but you can learn to perform the same services on a smaller scale.

AMERICAN ORT FEDERATION
817 Broadway, New York, NY 10003
(212) 677-4400

The American wing of an international Jewish *O*rganization for *R*ehabilitation and *T*raining, dedicated to providing vocational and technical education to Jewish people around the world.

Activities: ORT runs over 800 schools and training centers in 34 countries where more than 150,000 Jewish students—two-thirds of them teenagers—learn over 100 trades and skills; American ORT supervises the ORT schools in the United States, and is the primary fundraiser for the international organization.

Volunteer Opportunities: Mostly fundraising.

Contact: National headquarters.

"ORT builds dreams."

AMERICAN RED CROSS
17th & D Streets, NW, Washington, DC 20006
(202) 737–8300

The American Red Cross, a voluntary organization operating under congressional charter as part of the International Red Cross, works to improve the quality of human life; to enhance self-reliance and concern for others; and to help people avoid, prepare for, and cope with emergencies.

Activities: Operating throughout the U.S., it provides educational, health, social-welfare, and regular and emergency relief services.

Volunteer Opportunities: Governed, supported, and staffed mainly by some 1.5 million volunteers who work with paid staff in all programs and services—from fundraising to disaster relief—and who are coordinated in each community through volunteer chairpeople in line with personnel policies set by the national organization. Some activities require special training, which is provided, and some have a minimum-age requirement. However, the **Red Cross Youth Services** offer young people various special-service projects in school, in the community, and around the world; and leadership roles, including the planning and development of programs. It is also the place to learn skills that can be useful in other volunteer work and in careers.

Contact: National headquarters, or see phone book for local chapter. Check with local chapter to learn its specific needs.

> **"Red Cross volunteers not only help their communities and the world, but they themselves benefit from the enriching experiences and from the satisfaction that comes from helping others through an internationally respected organization that provides service to humanity."**

B'NAI B'RITH INTERNATIONAL
1640 Rhode Island Avenue, NW
Washington, DC 20036
(202) 857–6600

The world's largest Jewish-membership organization, providing educational, cultural, and social services to Jews and others in the United States and around the world.

Activities: Supports and protects Jews and Jewish rights throughout the world; sponsors youth organizations; provides community services for people of all faiths; maintains Anti-Defamation League to fight anti-Semitism; raises funds to support its activities and those of other groups it helps.

Volunteer Opportunities: Join youth organizations sponsored by group; participate in activities of any of organization's arms; help to raise funds. Membership open to Jews, but non-Jews welcome to help in community service.

Contact: National headquarters, or see phone book for local chapter.

> **"To strive for peace, decency, and justice for all the world's inhabitants—this is our program."**

CAMPAIGN FOR HUMAN DEVELOPMENT
1312 Massachusetts Avenue, NW
Washington, DC 20005
(202) 659-6650

Domestic social-service arm of the United States Catholic Conference, working to combat poverty and establish social justice in communities around the country.

Activities: Funds and coordinates social-service projects; produces educational materials; publicizes areas of concern; trains project leaders.

Volunteer Opportunities: None for the Campaign directly, but involvement needed in projects run in 175 regions.

Contact: National headquarters for location of nearest affiliate.

> **"Catholic social teaching demands concern and caring for one's neighbors. Volunteer involvement is a tangible expression of that concern."**

THE SALVATION ARMY

799 Bloomfield Avenue, Verona, NJ 07044
(201) 239–0606

An international religious and charitable movement organized to disseminate Christian ideas while providing social services to people of any creed.

Activities: Through service units around the country and the world, provides disaster relief; provides food, clothing, shelter, and health services to the needy; offers referrals to specialized services for alcoholics, addicts, prisoners, the elderly, and other groups; provides education and recreation programs for children and adults.

Volunteer Opportunities: Participate in most activities, including fundraising, according to needs of local centers.

Contact: National headquarters, or see phone book for nearest center.

"Compassion in action, through people helping people. Volunteers are the army behind the Army."

VOLUNTEERS OF AMERICA
3813 North Causeway Boulevard
Metairie, LA 70002
(504) 837–2652

A national nonprofit Christian human-service agency, providing 170 communities throughout the United States with multipurpose care programs.

Activities: Operates over 400 programs that serve the elderly, families, youth, offenders, drug abusers, alcoholics, and the disabled; cooperates with local businesses and service agencies; operates rehabilitation programs; raises funds to support its services.

Volunteer Opportunities: Vary according to local needs.

Contact: National headquarters, or see phone book for local chapter.

> **"For God and country—dedicated to helping Americans in need."**

PART
THREE

HOW TO VOLUNTEER

FOUR

WHAT A SUCCESSFUL VOLUNTEER NEEDS TO KNOW

Okay—you've gone through all the lists in this book, and you've come up with some terrific ideas for ways to lend your hand to some useful and satisfying project. Now what?

"Eighty-five percent of life is just showing up." That recipe for success is attributed to Woody Allen—and whoever said it, it's at least *ninety*-five percent true, especially when it comes to volunteering.

The groups who need your help need you, first of all, to show up. They can't use you—they can't do their work—if you don't.

And neither can you gain the benefits of volunteering if you're not there. Whether your personal goals for getting involved are, as we put it in Chapter 1, to "do good," to "feel good," to "look good," or to "better yourself," you have to *be* there to succeed.

This may seem more than obvious, but no-shows are the biggest problem that the volunteer coordinators for most organizations face. After all, they can't give you a raise for doing well, or fire you for slacking off—and they *do* rely on you.

Why is it such a problem? People tend to begin a volunteer project with tremendous enthusiasm and commitment—and then, too often, they just stop showing up. Maybe the work isn't what they thought it would be, maybe they don't have the time they thought they did, or maybe they find that they don't care as much about the cause as they thought.

So the first step toward being a successful volunteer is to choose a project that you *want* to show up for, and that you will *be able* to show up for.

The best way to do that is to look for volunteer work in the same way you would look for a job.

First, decide on the kind of work you want to do and why, then focus in on a few of the groups that seem most congenial. That's what all the listings and suggestions in this book will help you to do. And if you have *any* doubts about the validity or reputation of an organization, check it out: Talk with others who have worked for it; ask your local Chamber of Commerce, Better Business Bureau, or a related governmental agency for a rating of it. Next, call for an interview.

When you talk with the person who will "hire" you as a volunteer, you can expect to be asked

- why you want to perform this service,
- what you are capable of doing, and why,
- and why you have chosen this particular outlet for your skills and interests

In many organizations, the interview may be conducted just as though you were seeking paid work. (That's just one of the reasons why the volunteering experience can be so useful to your later life!)

In the interview, you will also need to get a lot of information for yourself. Here are the major points to cover.

ACTIVITIES—How well you do depends on doing what you

find satisfying, so make sure you know:

- What services are available for me to perform? (Refer to the descriptions in the lists here and in the organization's printed matter.)
- What is actually asked of me?
- Is training provided where necessary?
- Will these duties satisfy whatever community service requirements I need to fill? Will they satisfy my own interests?
- What am I willing to do? (Go back to your answers to the questions on page 8.)
- What am I *not* willing to do? (See "Drawing the Line," on page 136.)

TIME—Before you can promise to show up, you need to be sure that you can comfortably fit it into your schedule. So find out:

- How many hours per week are needed? (Remember to include travel time to and from the site.)
- How many hours do I actually have? (Remember that your schedule already includes school, homework, sports or club activities, family responsibilities, and time with friends.)
- *Which* hours do I have?
- How can I best fit my schedule into the needs of the group?

COSTS—Doing good usually isn't free, so you'll need to know:

- How much will it cost me to get to the site? (Remember transit fares, gas, and parking. Or, is transportation provided or paid?)
- If any kind of uniform is required, will it be provided?
- What other expenses might be involved? Will they be reimbursed?

Even if you don't have a formal interview, it's a good idea to visit the place where you'll be doing your volunteer work, and to meet the people who'll be supervising the project. When you do, keep your intuition alive and your antennae out: Does this seem like the kind of place in which you would be comfortable? Do the people seem congenial? There's no point in spending your free time unpleasantly, no matter how worthy the cause.

Once you and the organization decide that there is indeed a place for your services, you would do well to make only a tentative commitment: "I'm very interested in working with you, but I'd like to try it out for a while to be sure that I can do what you ask. I can promise to show up for three weeks, and then we'll see if it will work out for a longer time."

Most organizations will be happy to hear that kind of initial agreement, if only because it shows you're thoughtful. If they insist on a longer term, you'll be better off signing on somewhere else.

DRAWING THE LINE

Terrific! You've made a careful choice, and a commitment based on an honest appraisal of your skills and limitations. You show up as agreed and you provide the service you promised—and you're willing to take on varied tasks, especially since that's the best way to learn from your experience. You can reasonably expect to be treated fairly and with respect, right?

Unfortunately, this doesn't always happen. While we volunteers may wish to be greeted always with overwhelming gratitude for our services, we're sensible enough to be able to do without that. Sometimes, in fact, we're surprised to feel misused and even abused—and this may especially be true for *young* volunteers, whom some adults tend to boss around under any circumstances.

Just as we tend to assume, erroneously, that we must get involved only with the charitable motive of "doing good," we tend to expect that those who work for volunteer organizations have only big hearts, tolerance, and generous attitudes. The reality is that they are people just like any others. They may be underpaid, overworked, or dissatisfied with their positions. Or they may be driven, more than most, by the work they've felt called to do. The result can be frustration for the volunteer.

The most common problems that volunteers may encounter when they get involved are:

- Resentment from the paid personnel of the organization (They may look down on volunteers as not being "professional," or envy them for not having to "work for a living.")
- Demands for service beyond what was agreed (If you had a willing, free helping hand, you might ask for more, too.)
- Demands for service *beneath* what was agreed (Sweeping a hospital floor is not what you meant by "helping sick people.")

If you feel that you've showed your willingness to meet a group's expectations, but you run into this kind of problem where you are volunteering—or if you find that you can't fulfill your own original commitment of time or service—don't just yield to your temptation to simply disappear, even if you are *sure* that you are in the right. Rather, for your own sake and theirs, you can and should take some positive action: Talk about the difficulty to someone in charge and see if you can improve the situation. If you can't, you can feel free to give notice and leave.

A writer who volunteered to do writing and publicity for a city agency found that he didn't really like the woman he worked with but felt he had to fulfill his commitment. When she began to ask him to do typing and other clerical duties rather than to write, he reminded her of what services he had offered to perform. It was only after she pulled rank on him, as though he was her employee, that he "resigned." He was annoyed and disappointed, he said, but from the experience he had gained some knowledge about himself, the world, and the way to handle similar situations in the future, whether as a volunteer or as a paid worker.

Even if you have to leave a volunteer involvement, if you handle it in a mature and businesslike way, you haven't wasted your time or your energy. Though you may not have the satisfactions you expected, you have learned from the experience.

HAPPY ENDINGS

When your volunteer experience comes to a *successful* conclusion, be sure to get the best long-term effects from it. Ask for a letter of recommendation. Many well-organized groups will provide one automatically, but if yours doesn't, ask for one from someone in charge. If you feel embarrassed, or think it's not worth the trouble, read these excerpts from actual letters written for teen volunteers:

> ". . . responsible, hardworking and quick to learn . . . she reorganized our filing system, learned our computer system, and helped with numerous mailings. . . . one of the finest volunteers I have had the pleasure to work with."

> ". . . an outstanding individual, [she] was a valuable asset to our volunteer program. . . . a self-starter, enthusiastic and sensitive . . ."

> ". . . he was involved in computerizing statistics . . . with boundless creativity and energy . . . his efforts were largely responsible for us meeting our deadline."

Wouldn't you like to have that kind of comment in the portfolio you show to colleges or future employers? Well worth the effort!

Schools that require community service usually require participants to submit some kind of written report on their experience. Even if yours doesn't, or if you're volunteering on your own, this is not a bad idea for you, either. Writing about your project can clarify it for you, keep it real for now and the future. Do an article for the school paper or magazine perhaps—or use it as the theme for a class essay. Or make notes in a journal, or simply write a letter to yourself, the people you worked with, or a friend—even if that "sounds like work," it will be well worth the effort, too. You'll be glad to have a written record to which you can refer later, when you may well want to include the details on applications for colleges or jobs, or to get in touch with your supervisors for references or employment leads.

The suggestions (and warnings) in this chapter aren't meant to discourage you from getting involved but to make your experience, whatever it may be, a worthwhile one.

Still, if reading this makes volunteering seem too much like work, check the next chapter for some alternate ways to satisfy your very human need to get involved.

FIVE

MORE WAYS TO LEND YOUR HAND

If you realize that you can't or don't want to get involved as an individual on a long-term basis with an organized volunteer group, you can still find ways to satisfy that urge to do good. Here are some suggestions.

SHORT-TERM SHARING

- Watch for one-shot special events, like Hands Across America, or the walk-a-thons, bike-a-thons, read-a-thons, or other annual fundraising activities sponsored by both local and national groups. They're fun and require only one day of commitment. You can learn of this kind of event through radio and television announcements, ads in newspapers and newsletters, or posters placed around town and in libraries, community centers, and other public places. So when you hear of a special public service activity that sounds intriguing, give it a try: It's not only "other people" who enjoy this easy kind of goodwill participation.

- You needn't even give of yourself to lend a hand to those in need: A donation of usable goods to a helping organization can give you a good feeling with a minimum of work. You probably are uncomfortably aware that someone can use those outgrown clothes, books, or games that cram your room or closet. You're right—and it's easy to pass them on. Just sort through them and take the ones that still have some life left to a local charity thrift shop, shelter for the homeless, or other worthy organization. Or, deposit them in one of the receptacles that Goodwill Industries has placed around many neighborhood shopping malls. It's no big deal, but the "thank you" is well worth the effort. On a larger scale, you can also take part in organizing a drive to collect donations—food at Thanksgiving, toys at Christmas—or stage a community closet cleaning for goods to go to Goodwill or the Salvation Army, or similar groups.
- At holiday time—not just the major winter celebrations, but every holiday—organizations are always in need of many extra hands for their special activities. You could help with Thanksgiving dinner for the poor, or trick-or-treat for UNICEF, or accompany a group of old people or children to the beach on Memorial Day. Look for notices in newspapers, neighborhood bulletin boards, and newsletters, and ask the community service, health, and religious organizations in your area when it is, throughout the year, that they need extra help. You can also leave your name and number with these groups, so that when they need helping hands, they can call on you. With that arrangement, you can always say "no," but you have lots of opportunities to say "yes."
- On a less pleasant note, disasters and emergencies are also times when short-term volunteer aid is needed. You can collect food and clothing for victims of a faraway earthquake, or help to clean up after a local fire or flood. Often, calls for help are broadcast and published at these times of urgent need, whether local, national, or international, and you can be ready to re-

spond to the addresses or numbers included in these announcements. Or, you can present yourself at the firehouse, Red Cross office, or emergency station to let the other volunteers there know that you are ready to lend a hand.

It's a good feeling—and who knows? You might want to make a habit of helping out.

STRENGTH IN NUMBERS

You may find a cause that you find important, but you can't commit enough time to it on your own. You are surrounded by groups of people who are looking for service projects. Suggest your idea to: your student council, school clubs, community or block associations, or youth organizations that you belong to or know of, such as the Scouts, 4-H, or religion-affiliated groups. A New York City student found herself particularly moved by stories of missing children but felt she could do little on her own. So she enlisted the aid of her Girls' Club in a campaign that raised funds for a national child-tracing organization, and raised awareness of the problem among students in area schools. Her efforts also gained media attention (the press always likes a story about a "little guy" taking on a big problem), so its effectiveness was multiplied still further.

When you're inspired in that way, go to an organization with which you're familiar and lobby for your idea: Using the same material that stirred *you* to action, tell the group leaders what needs doing, why it needs doing, and how they can benefit by helping. Many clubs, of both adults and youths, are happy to be handed a new project that needs their joint efforts, so you'll probably succeed. And if you do, you'll be called on to help out yourself, of course, but you'll be part of a pool of energy and talent, so you won't need to have so much time available.

GROUP IT YOURSELF

If no group exists to address a problem that concerns you, you can organize your own or your own local chapter of a larger organization.

That can be a terrific experience on many levels, because not only are you doing good for a cause you care about, but you also learn firsthand about leadership and working with others. As you might imagine, this kind of experience can also be rigorous, so here are some suggestions for going about it.

- Find others who share your interest.
- Pick people who are energetic and reliable.
- Put your group's purpose and organization in writing.
- Start *small:* Rather than collecting extra food for the homeless in the whole city, for example, focus on one grocery store or deli that is willing to distribute leftovers to the needy in one neighborhood.
- Assign responsibilities sensibly: The member who can write or has access to a photocopy machine should handle publicity, for instance; the one with best access to local businesses should make those contacts, and so forth.
- Let the press know about what you're doing, since media attention is a great way to recruit volunteers and get business support. Send notices to local newspapers and radio and television news bureaus, then phone them. Make it clear that this is a group of *young people* who are taking on an important community problem: That's called a "man bites dog" piece, which is of special appeal to the press. (You'll find guides to getting press attention at your library—ask the librarian.)
- Reach out to local businesses for financial and other kinds of support. Present your project clearly—and be sure to include an explanation of what's in it for them!
- Get advice and direct help from existing organizations and from books and resources listed on pages 149–152.

AT LONG DISTANCE
Many people find great satisfaction, at little cost of time or

energy, in corresponding with people in need. Even if your schedule is tight, you might enjoy writing to a prisoner, "adopting" an impoverished child abroad, writing lobby letters for a social-action group, or visiting a hospital or nursing-home patient periodically.

THE UNLISTED

Whatever your special needs or interests, no matter how unique you may feel, there probably exists a group somewhere that shares them and would appreciate your involvement, even if you haven't found mention of it in this book. We haven't listed hobby groups, for example, or self-help organizations. In fact, there are thousands of groups that aren't included here, in part because of the narrowness of their appeal. And there are undoubtedly hundreds of thousands of other groups, especially on the local level, that aren't listed in any publication. So don't give up!

Instead, check out the suggestions in Chapter 7 for even more ways to get involved.

SIX

TO ADULTS: USING YOUNG HANDS

Energy. That's what you're dealing with if you're involved with young people. And if you're involved with a voluntary organization in need of help, that's what you can tap.

If each of the suggested activities in this book were taken up by only one teenager, just imagine the changes that they could work in their lives, in their communities, and in the world: That's the kind of energy you have available.

"WHAT DO I DO WITH THEM?"
Adolescent energy is often the despair of the adults who teach, lead, or counsel teenagers. Too often, we adults try (without much success) to control that energy, to keep it in check—while at the same time trying to keep teens away from drug abuse, crime, promiscuity, and other destructive behavior.

Some of the benefits of the constructive channeling of that energy are obvious: Time after time it has been shown that when we allow and encourage young people to be and feel useful, to take on adult responsibilities, to express themselves and explore their world in positive ways, we don't have to work so hard at keeping them away from negative behavior.

There are some more pragmatic benefits as well.

If you are a school **teacher** or **administrator,** you should know that a strong voluntary-service program in your school can win and maintain the important support of your community. (And can win awards for your school, too!) Experiential learning through volunteer work can reinforce and make meaningful (and therefore memorable) the learning that goes on in the classroom. Also, when your students—who already feel like adults—are encouraged to participate in society as adults, they are more likely to *act* like adults in school.

If you are a youth **group leader** or **adviser,** you will find, as your colleagues have, that a volunteer project can enhance group feeling and provide a cohesiveness in ways that no socializing or busywork can match.

Adolescent **counselors** see individual teens grow in self-esteem and ability to relate when they can reach out beyond themselves and help someone else.

The means to achieving these good ends are really quite simple: Make the opportunities available to the young people in your life, and show them the benefits of participation. That's what this book attempts to do, and you can help teens follow through on some of the suggestions included here.

Make use of the resource organizations listed on pages 150–152, as well. You'll get effective tips, including ways to check out organizations that want to employ teens as volunteers, and techniques for supervising and enhancing their activities.

It's important that young volunteers be involved in work that excites *them*, but you can help them to start their own projects by, perhaps, suggesting areas that need filling. Also, you can serve as a liaison with existing social-service agencies, or with local businesses that could support youth-sponsored projects.

And in the process of all this, you'll find that *you* are getting involved, too—and if you didn't know them before, you'll learn firsthand the benefits of lending a hand.

"HOW CAN I MAKE THEM WORK FOR ME?"

If your job is to administer a nonprofit organization, you likely are worried about today's dearth of adult volunteers—so why not turn to teens? Anxiety over the problems of the world, a concern for career success, a desire for something *more* from life—for teenagers, those feelings are often even more intense than they are for the rest of us. That's why young people can be an outstanding resource for you as an **organizer** or **administrator** of volunteer projects.

Yet, surprisingly, they are a resource frequently overlooked by voluntary organizations, even when volunteers are in short supply. The research questionnaire for this book, for example, asked each organization if it had any "age requirements" for volunteers. Many of the groups responding assumed that the question referred to *maximum* ages, but on further inquiry they said that yes, they could use teenagers.

On the other hand, some of this country's major associations not only use teenagers but make special provisions for young volunteers, either by establishing youth-oriented projects within their programs, or by appointing volunteer coordinators solely for the young. (See, for instance, the entries for American Red Cross and March of Dimes.)

A group may ignore adolescents as volunteer prospects because they believe the bad press that teenagers have commonly received. You're likely to find, however, as many organizations can confirm, that when expectations for teen volunteers are spelled out as carefully as they are for adults, the young are at least as reliable and productive as the rest—and they have all that *energy*!

The use of minors as volunteers may require some special

considerations, especially in reference to insurance regulations or local laws, but if you're both cautious and creative, it's worth the effort.

And how do you tap this vast source of human energy? Reach out to them where they are—in their groups and through what they read and (constantly) listen to. Like the rest of us, young people want success, satisfaction, and something different or exciting in their lives. So you'll need to present your organization and the work it does as not only an adventure but an *important* adventure.

And who knows? While you're figuring out how to go about this, you may gain a new, rewarding perspective on yourself, your work, and your *own* life goals.

Whether you're a teen counselor or a volunteer organizer, you're wise never to underestimate the energy of adolescents. Often, all you'll need to do to tap that energy is to point out some projects where they are needed, and they will enthusiastically lend their hands.

SEVEN

CHECK IT OUT

Still looking for valuable ways to lend your hand? There are *many* others. Here are some easy-to-find sources for information. They should lead you to the activity that's just right for *you*.

BOOKS AND DIRECTORIES

Encyclopedia of Associations. Gale Research Co., annual.

A 3-volume annual directory listing some 24,000 national and international organizations by topic, describing their activities and membership and providing addresses and phone numbers for each. Available at most libraries, and worth searching for.

The Telephone Directory.

The Yellow Pages in the phone books of all but the smallest of towns include various categories of voluntary organizations (for instance, "Associations," "Social-Service Organizations," or "Volunteer") that list all the groups active in the region. Here also are specific entries, like "Hospitals," or "Animal . . ." . And check the White Pages under "Volunteer" and "Voluntary."

The phone book also has a section of government listings that includes general information numbers and numbers for voluntary-action or social-service agencies.

Larger public libraries have available regional phone books and those for the cities in the area.

Volunteer! Council on International Educational Exchange, 1984.
A guide, regularly revised, to opportunities for voluntary service, with a focus on work camps and overseas programs.

OTHER RESOURCES

The following organizations can provide information on volunteering in general, direction to specific volunteer activities, or both.

National

ACTION
806 Connecticut Avenue, NW
Washington, DC 20525
(202) 634–9108
An agency of the federal government that administers such nationwide volunteer activities as VISTA (Volunteers in Service to America), and can provide information and referrals for various social-service volunteer projects.

Campus Outreach Opportunity League ("COOL")
180 18th Street, NW
Washington, DC 20006
(202) 783–8855
Coordinating clearinghouse for a network of volunteer activities on college campuses and in some high schools around

the country. Publishes a community service resource book for students and provides information and ideas.

Father Flanagan's Boys' Home
Communications & Public Service Division
Boys Town, NE 68010
Publishes a useful and thorough directory of U.S. youth organizations whose activities encompass a full range of religious, social, political, and self-help activities.

Independent Sector
1828 L Street, NW
Washington, DC 20036
(202) 223–8100
Private coalition of 650 nonprofit organizations nationwide with goal of promoting voluntary service. Offers a guidebook to youth-service programs and can provide referrals to member organizations in need of volunteers.

National Association of Secondary School Principals
1904 Association Drive
Reston, VA 22091
(703) 860–0200
Through its Division of Student Activities and The National Honor Society, which it sponsors, provides ideas and information on student volunteering in public and private high schools.

VOLUNTEER—The National Center
1111 North 19th Street
Arlington, VA 22209
(703) 276–0542
Private nonprofit coordinating organization for the promotion of effective volunteering nationwide. Produces publi-

cations and can provide referrals to voluntary-action centers in local areas.

Local

In your community, many **private groups** are already involved with voluntary service; you might want to join them, get ideas from them, or use them for your own projects. They include youth groups like Scouting organizations, CYO, Hillel and service-oriented clubs like Lions or Kiwanis. Your local office of The United Way can also provide a list of member organizations in need of volunteers.

Most cities, counties, and states have **public agencies** for coordinating voluntary activities in both public and private service.

The **public library** in most communities maintains a file of local groups that need volunteers, and has available the directories referred to in this section. Librarians themselves are an excellent resource for information and ideas.

So check it out—then lend your hand.

LIST OF ORGANIZATIONS

INDEX